KALLIS' iBT TOEFL® PATTERN

Speaking 3

TOEFL® is a registered trademark of Educational Testing Services (ETS), Princeton, New Jersey, USA. The content in this text, including the practice prompts, Model Answer, and Hacking Strategy, is created and designed exclusively by KALLIS. This publication is not endorsed or approved by ETS.

KALLIS' iBT TOEFL® Pattern Speaking 3

KALLIS EDU, INC.
7490 Opportunity Road, Suite 203
San Diego, CA 92111
(858) 277-8600
info@kallisedu.com
www.kallisedu.com

Copyright © 2014 KALLIS EDU, INC.

All rights reserved. No part of this book may be reproduced, stored in a retrieval system, or transmitted in any form or by any means, electronic or mechanical, including photocopying, recording, or otherwise, without the prior written permission of the copyright owner.

ISBN-10: 1-5058-8145-5
ISBN-13: 978-1-5058-8145-8

iBT TOEFL® Pattern - Speaking III is the third of our three-level iBT TOEFL® Speaking Exam preparation book series.

Our **iBT TOEFL® Pattern Speaking** series simplifies each TOEFL speaking task into a series of simple steps, which ensures that students do not become overwhelmed as they develop their speaking skills. Moreover, our commitment to minimizing instruction and maximizing student practice assures that students have many opportunities to strengthen their speaking skills.

KALLIS

KALLIS'

TOEFL® iBT
PATTERN
SPEAKING 3
PERFECTION

Getting Started

A study guide should familiarize the reader with the material found on the test, develop unique methods that can be used to solve various question types, and provide practice questions to challenge future test-takers. *KALLIS' iBT TOEFL® Pattern Series* aims to accomplish all these study tasks by presenting iBT TOEFL® test material in an organized, comprehensive, and easy-to-understand way.

KALLIS' iBT TOEFL® Pattern Speaking Series provides in-depth explanations and practices that will help you prepare for the iBT TOEFL speaking section. This study guide focuses on the development of simple, step-by-step response strategies that will guide you when responding to each speaking task.

Understanding the Speaking Tasks

Chapters 1 through 6 are devoted to explaining and solving each of the six speaking tasks. The beginning of each of these chapters introduces one of the six types of speaking tasks encountered on the iBT TOEFL speaking section. These introductory sections will prepare you for the explanations and practices that follow.

General Information

The **General Information** section presents the speaking skills that you will need to complete the speaking portion of the iBT TOEFL and provides descriptions of each speaking task.

Hacking Strategy

The **Hacking Strategy** and corresponding **Example** provide a step-by-step process that explains how to prepare for and respond to each speaking task. While the **Hacking Strategy** develops a common process that can be used to respond to any speaking task, the **Example** demonstrates how this common process can be used to solve one particular type of speaking task.

Improving Speaking Skills through Practice

A combination of explanations and practices breaks down each speaking task into simple, step-by-step processes.

Practices

In Chapters 1 through 6, each step of the **Hacking Strategy** is elaborated on with a brief explanation and with five or more **Practices**. These provide opportunities to develop the skills that you just read about. Each **Practice** builds upon information presented earlier in the chapter, allowing you to gradually develop skills that you will use when you are responding to the speaking tasks.

Actual Practice

Chapter 7 consists of six **Actual Practices**, which provide templates to help you outline and compose Independent and Integrated speaking responses. Thus, **Actual Practices** require you to use skills from all **Practices**, so **Actual Practices** should be attempted only after you are familiar with the structure of the iBT TOEFL speaking section.

Actual Test

The **Actual Test** section, which is located in Chapter 8, presents all six speaking tasks in a format that resembles the official iBT TOEFL speaking test. This section should be attempted only after all speaking skills have been mastered.

In Case You Need Help

▶ At the end of Chapters 1 through 6, you will find **Speaking Task Checklists**. In the beginning of Chapter 7, you will find an **Independent** and **Integrated Speaking Task Rubric**. Reviewing these before you begin speaking can help you structure your responses; reviewing them after you have completed a speaking task can help you assess the quality of your responses.

▶ A **Model Answer** is located after each **Practice**. These **Model Answers** demonstrate one acceptable way to respond to each prompt, but there will often be many acceptable responses for any given task. So do not feel that your responses must be the same as the **Model Answers**; just use them for guidance when necessary.

Table of Contents

INDEPENDENT SPEAKING

Chapter 1

Sharing a Personal Experience

General Background Information	2
Hacking Strategy	4
Practice 1	7
Practice 2	9
Practice 3	11
Practice 4	13
Practice 5	15
Practice 6	17
Practice 7	19
Practice 8	21
Practice 9	23
Practice 10	25
Checklist	27

Chapter 2

Selecting a Preference

General Background Information	30
Hacking Strategy	32
Practice 1	35
Practice 2	37
Practice 3	39
Practice 4	41
Practice 5	43
Practice 6	45
Practice 7	47
Practice 8	49
Practice 9	51
Practice 10	53
Checklist	55

INTEGRATED SPEAKING

Chapter 3

Campus Situation

General Background Information	58
Hacking Strategy	59
Practice 1	62
Practice 2	66
Practice 3	70
Practice 4	74
Practice 5	78
Checklist	82

Chapter 4

Academic Course

General Background Information	84
Hacking Strategy	85
Practice 1	88
Practice 2	92
Practice 3	96
Practice 4	100
Practice 5	104
Checklist	108

SPEAKING 3 PERFECTION

Ready, set, speak!

Chapter 5

Campus Situation

General Background Information	110
Hacking Strategy	111
Practice 1	114
Practice 2	118
Practice 3	122
Practice 4	126
Practice 5	130
Checklist	134

Chapter 6

Academic Course

General Background Information	136
Hacking Strategy	137
Practice 1	140
Practice 2	144
Practice 3	148
Practice 4	152
Practice 5	156
Checklist	160

Chapter 7

Actual Practice

Actual Practice 1	166
Actual Practice 2	186
Actual Practice 3	206
Actual Practice 4	226
Actual Practice 5	246
Actual Practice 6	266

Chapter 8

Actual Test   288

Before You Begin...

INDEPENDENT AND INTEGRATED TASKS

The iBT TOEFL Speaking test consists of six tasks: two Independent tasks and four Integrated tasks.

The first two tasks are called "Independent tasks" because they require you to produce a response without using any extra written or spoken materials. Thus, you must come up with responses to the first two tasks independently, using your own experiences or opinions.

The last four tasks are called "Integrated tasks" because they require you to incorporate, or integrate, material from spoken and/or written sources into your response. Task 3, for example, will require you to read a passage, listen to a conversation, and then form a response based on what you have read and heard. Two of the Integrated tasks deal with university-related issue, and the other two Integrated tasks discuss academic topics that reflect material that an American-university student might encounter.

TRANSITION WORDS AND PHRASES

Transition words and phrases explain how the content of one sentence relates to the rest of your response.

Meaning	Examples
addition	*additionally, furthermore, in addition, in fact, moreover*
cause-and-effect	*as a result, consequently, then, therefore, to this end*
compare/contrast	*compared to, despite, however, in contrast, on the contrary, on the one hand, on the other hand, nevertheless*
conclusions	*finally, in conclusion, in summary, lastly, thus, in short*
examples	*for example, for instance, in this case, in this situation*
introductions	*according to, as indicated in/by, based on*
reasons	*one reason is, another reason is, due to*
sequence	*afterward, again, also, and, finally, first, next, previously, second, third*

SYMBOLS AND ABBREVIATIONS

When writing down notes to prepare for a spoken response, save time by using symbols instead of words. In addition to using the symbols in the chart below, you can create your own symbols.

Symbol	Meaning	Symbol	Meaning
&	and	=	equals, is
%	percent	>	more than
#	number	<	less than
@	at	→	resulting in
↓	decreasing	↑	increasing

ABBREVIATIONS FOR UNIVERSITY ACTIVITIES

Abbreviation	Meaning	Abbreviation	Meaning
edu.	education	RA	resident assistant
GE	general education	stu.	student
GPA	grade point average	TA	teaching assistant
prof.	professor/professional	univ.	university

ABBREVIATIONS FOR ACADEMIC TOPICS

Abbreviation	Meaning	Abbreviation	Meaning
bio.	biology/biological	exp.	experience/experiment
c.	century	info.	information
chem.	chemistry/chemical	gov.	government
def.	definition	hyp.	hypothesis
econ.	economics/economy	phys.	physics/physical
env.	environment	psych.	psychology/psychological
ex.	example	sci.	science/scientific

OTHER ABBREVIATIONS

Abbreviation	Meaning	Abbreviation	Meaning
abt.	about	pic.	picture
b/c	because	ppl.	people
comm.	community/communication	pref.	preference
e/o	each other	pt.	point
fam.	family	ques.	question
fav.	favorite	s/b	somebody
gen.	general/generation	s/o	someone
hr.	hour	sec.	second
impt.	important	w/	with
loc.	location	w/i	within
lvl.	level	w/o	without
min.	minute	yr.	year

iBT TOEFL Speaking Task Composition

Task Type	Task Description	Time (Total 20 Minutes)
Independent Tasks		
1. Independent Task <Personal Opinion Task>	Speak about your opinion regarding people, places, events, or activities	Preparation Time: 15 Sec Answer Time: 45 Sec
2. Independent Task <Personal Preference Task>	Choose one of two opposing views, and defend your choice	Preparation Time: 15 Sec Answer Time: 45 Sec
Integrated Tasks Read/Listen/Speak		
3. Integrated Task <Campus Situation>	*Reading: an announcement regarding a campus-related issue (75-100 words) *Listening: a conversation regarding the announcement (60-80 seconds) *Responding: summarize the announcement and give the speaker's opinion on the issue	Preparation Time: 30 Sec Answer Time: 60 Sec
4. Integrated Task <Academic Course Topic>	*Reading: terminology or definition of an academic subject (75-100 words) *Listening: a lecture giving specific information about the terminology or concept (60-90 seconds) *Responding: address the prompt, often by summarizing the reading and the listening	Preparation Time: 30 Sec Answer Time: 60 Sec
Integrated Tasks Listen/Speak		
5. Integrated Task <Campus Situation>	*Listening: a conversation that presents a student's and two possible solutions (60-90 minutes) *Responding: summarize the problem, state your preferred solution, and support your preference with reasons and details	Preparation Time: 20 Sec Answer Time: 60 Sec
6. Integrated Task <Academic Course Topic>	*Listening: a lecture that explains a term or concept using specific examples. (90-120 minutes) *Responding: summarize the lecture and show an understanding of the topic and its details	Preparation Time: 20 Sec Answer Time: 60 Sec

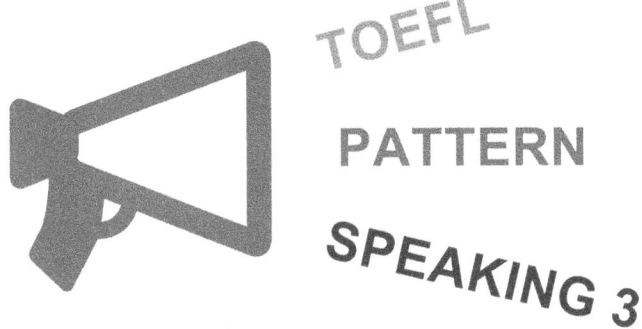

CHAPTER 1

Sharing a Personal Experience

Sharing a Personal Experience

GENERAL BACKGROUND INFORMATION

1. EXPLANATION OF TASK 1

Speaking Task 1 asks you to speak about a personal experience or familiar topic. A narrator will read the prompt aloud; the prompt will stay on the computer screen during your preparation and response times.

You will then have 15 seconds to prepare your response. Begin preparing when the "Preparation Time" notice appears on your screen. Use the time to write down a few notes in outline form because you will not have enough time to write a full answer.

At the end of 15 seconds, you will hear a short beep. The "Preparation Time" notice changes to "Response Time." The countdown from 45 seconds begins. Your response will be recorded during the 45 seconds. At the end, the recording will stop. A new screen will indicate that the response time has ended.

2. NECESSARY SKILLS FOR TASK 1

You must be able to:

- recall personal experiences and events and form opinions about them
- organize ideas coherently with a clear topic statement and supporting reasons
- speak clearly using correct grammar, vocabulary, and pronunciation

3. EXPLANATION OF QUESTION TYPES

You will see one of two types of questions for the personal experience prompt. In both types of prompt, you must state an opinion and support that opinion with reasons and details.

> **Question Types**
>
> **1 Describing a Familiar Person, Place, Activity, or Event**
>
> Describe X. Explain how X has affected your life. Use specific reasons and details to support your answer.
>
> **2 Expressing Personal Likes, Dislikes, or Values**
>
> Describe your favorite/least favorite X. Explain why X is your favorite/least favorite. Use specific reasons and examples to support your answer.

4. EXAMPLE PROMPTS

Possible Task 1 prompts that you may encounter on the official TOEFL exam include:

> **Prompt**
>
> - Describe a city or town where you have lived. Explain why you believe that it is either a good or bad place to live. Use specific reasons and details to support your answer.
>
> - What is one subject that you think every high school student should be required to study? Explain why you believe that this subject is important. Give reasons for your answer.
>
> - What is your favorite day of the week? Explain what makes it your favorite day. Include reasons and details to support your answer.
>
> - Describe a time when you have worked with a group to complete a challenging assignment or task. Use details to support your answer.
>
> - Describe the most interesting trip that you have taken. Explain what made this trip so interesting. Support your answer with reasons and details.
>
> - What do you think would be the biggest challenge of running your own company? Explain your answer using specific reasons and details.

5. USEFUL EXPRESSIONS

Some useful expressions for Task 1 are:

- I think (that) _____.

- I believe (that) _____.

- In my experience, _____.

- The most _____ is _____ because _____.

- The best _____ is _____ because _____.

- The worst _____ is _____ because _____.

- My favorite _____ is _____ because _____.

- My least favorite _____ is _____ because _____.

HACKING STRATEGY

STEP 1. OUTLINE YOUR RESPONSE

- Read the prompt carefully
- Decide on an opinion

STEP 2. PREPARE YOUR RESPONSE

- Make your opinion into a topic statement
- Add reasons that support your opinion

STEP 3. DELIVER YOUR RESPONSE

- Respond using coherent sentences
- Add transition words between ideas

EXAMPLE 1

STEP 1. OUTLINE YOUR RESPONSE

As you read and listen to the prompt, start outlining a response that includes two details or examples that support your opinion.

> **Prompt**
> With whom do you usually enjoy talking? What makes the conversation with this person so enjoyable? Use specific reasons and examples to support your answer.

First, form an opinion that responds to the question that the prompt is asking you to address.

- **Opinion:** *talk to sister*

STEP 2. PREPARE YOUR RESPONSE

When organizing your response, you should make your opinion into a topic statement and come up with at least two reasons or details that support your topic statement. Because you are only given 15 seconds to prepare for your response, you must organize your thoughts quickly.

- **Topic Statement:** *One of the people I love talking with is my sister.*
  - **Reason 1:** *understand e/o: express feelings / relax, trust*
  - **Reason 2:** *knowledgeable: older, good @ explaining/interesting, relaxing*

STEP 3. DELIVER YOUR RESPONSE

Use the outline that you created in STEP 2 to guide you as you deliver your response. Respond using complete sentences, and add transition words to show how ideas relate to one another.

> *One of the people I love talking with is my sister. There are two main reasons for this.* **One reason** *is that we know each other so well that we can relate to each other and understand each other's feelings. When we talk, we have the feeling of understanding and being understood, which allows us to relax and trust the other person.* **Another reason** *I enjoy talking with my sister is that she's knowledgeable in so many different subjects. She's older than I am, so she can usually explain difficult concepts and tell me things that I didn't know before. That makes talking with her interesting as well as relaxing.*

EXAMPLE 2

STEP 1. OUTLINE YOUR RESPONSE

As you read and listen to the prompt, start outlining a response that includes two details or examples that support your opinion.

> **Prompt**
> What do you miss the most when you are away from home? Include details and examples to support your explanation.

First, decide on one or two things that you miss when you are away from home.

- **Opinion:** *miss my puppy & mom's food*

STEP 2. PREPARE YOUR RESPONSE

When organizing your response, you should make your opinion into a topic statement and come up with at least two reasons or details that support your topic statement. Because you are only given 15 seconds to prepare for your response, you must organize your thoughts quickly.

- **Topic Statement:** *There are two things I miss the most when I'm away from home. One is my puppy, and the other is my mom's delicious food.*
- **Reason 1:** *my puppy: 5 yrs. old, friendly*
- **Reason 2:** *mom's food: grow vege. → healthy, best taste*

STEP 3. DELIVER YOUR RESPONSE

Use the outline that you created in STEP 2 to guide you as you deliver your response. Respond using complete sentences, and add transition words to show how ideas relate to one another.

There are two things I miss the most when I'm away from home. One is my puppy, and the other is my mom's delicious food. **First of all**, *my puppy is one of my best friends. I've had him for almost 5 years now, and he's always been friendly to me. He's never gotten aggressive toward me or anyone else. So every time I'm away from home, I really miss him a lot.* **The next thing** *I miss is my mom's delicious food. And not only is her food delicious, but it's also healthy: she uses home-grown vegetables harvested freshly from our garden. When I'm away from home, I can never find vegetables that are as delicious as the ones my mom grows.*

Task 1

Practice 1 — Your Turn

Question 1 of 6

Describe a time in your life when you helped a friend or family member. How did you help them? Use specific details to support your answer.

Preparation Time 00:00:15
Response Time   00:00:45

Notes

Opinion: _____

_____

_____

_____

_____

Response

_____

_____

_____

_____

_____

_____

_____

_____

_____

Task 1

Practice 1 — Model Answer

Question 1 of 6

Describe a time in your life when you helped a friend or family member. How did you help them? Use specific details to support your answer.

Notes

Opinion: _@ cousin's wedding_

1) other cousin's children → restless
   - took them to store → snacks
   - "indoor picnic"

 Response

One time that I helped a family member was at my cousin's wedding. I was a teenager, and I was just sitting there while my aunt and my mom were going crazy getting the bride and everyone else ready. As the time for the ceremony came closer, my other cousin's children began to cry. They were tired and bored, and no one had remembered to feed them lunch. So my aunt gave me some money to go to a convenience store and get some snacks for them. Then I said to the kids, "Let's have an indoor picnic," and we sat on the carpet and ate. The kids were able to calmly take part in the wedding after that, and I felt good to have helped.

Task 1

Practice 2 — **Your Turn**

Question 1 of 6

What is your favorite season of the year? Explain why you like this season so much. Include reasons and details to support your answer.

Preparation Time 00:00:15
Response Time 00:00:45

Notes

Opinion: _____

_____

_____

_____

_____

Response

Practice 2 — Model Answer

Question 1 of 6

What is your favorite season of the year? Explain why you like this season so much. Include reasons and details to support your answer.

Notes

Opinion: _winter_

1) hate hot: summer → sweaty
   - not easily affected by cold

2) winter sport (ski)
   - speeding down = spectacular

 Response

Although every season has some benefits, my absolute favorite season is winter. First, I don't really like summer very much because I can't tolerate the heat. During summertime, I get hot and sweaty, which makes me feel horrible. As a result, I avoid doing any physical activity in the summer, which I know must be bad for my health. But in winter, nothing bothers me because I'm not easily affected by the cold. In addition, I like winter because I can do some activities that I can't do in other seasons. I particularly love skiing during the winter months. Speeding down the steep, snow-covered mountains is a spectacular activity, and it's only possible in winter.

Task 1

Practice 3  **Your Turn**

Question 1 of 6

Describe your ideal job. Explain why the job would be perfect for you. Include specific details to support your answer.

 Preparation Time 00:00:15
Response Time 00:00:45

Notes

Opinion: _____

_____

_____

_____

_____

Response

_____

_____

_____

_____

_____

_____

_____

_____

_____

Task 1

Practice 3 — Model Answer

Question 1 of 6

Describe your ideal job. Explain why the job would be perfect for you. Include specific details to support your answer.

Notes

Opinion: _human rights lawyer_

1) ex. poor regions
   - children work long hrs., paid little
   - bad working env. → accidents

2) my job → help oppressed, improve conditions

 Response

My ideal job is to be a human rights lawyer. I think this would be a perfect job for me because I've always had an interest in human rights issues. For one, almost every country has regions where human rights are ignored. In some countries, children are forced to work long hours to support their families, yet they're paid very little. Moreover, in these same workplaces, bad working conditions lead to many workplace accidents. Therefore, knowing that these serious issues exist, I strongly believe it's my job to protect these people. I want to become a human rights lawyer who can help the oppressed and improve their terrible working and living conditions.

Task 1

Practice 4 — **Your Turn**

Question 1 of 6

Describe a job that you would never want to do. Explain why you would not want to do this job. Use specific reasons and examples to support your answer.

Preparation Time 00:00:15
Response Time 00:00:45

Notes

Opinion: _____

Response

Task 1

Practice 4 — *Model Answer*

Question 1 of 6

Describe a job that you would never want to do. Explain why you would not want to do this job. Use specific reasons and examples to support your answer.

Notes

Opinion: _doctor_

1) work too much
 - TV → doctors always busy, emergencies

2) too much stress
 - have to determine life or death

 Response

I'd never want to be a doctor for a number of reasons. First of all, I think doctors work too many hours. For example, when I watch television programs set in hospitals, doctors always seem to be rushing from one place to another. There are emergencies everywhere, and doctors end up spending too much time at work. I have hobbies outside of work, so this wouldn't be a good job for me. Second, doctors deal with too much stress. They make decisions that determine whether people live or die. They see patients every day who are unstable. I'm a very sensitive person, so this type of stress would be impossible for me to handle.

Task 1

Practice 5 — Your Turn

Question 1 of 6

Choose one extreme sport from the list below that you would most like to try. Explain why you think it would be an enjoyable activity. If none appeals to you, explain why.

- Skydiving
- Rock climbing
- Hang gliding

Preparation Time 00:00:15
Response Time   00:00:45

Notes

Opinion: _____

_____

_____

_____

_____

Response

Task 1

Practice 5 — Model Answer

Question 1 of 6

Choose one extreme sport from the list below that you would most like to try. Explain why you think it would be an enjoyable activity. If none appeals to you, explain why.
- Skydiving
- Rock climbing
- Hang gliding

Notes

Opinion: _rock climbing_

1) always loved to climb
   - climbed trees, roof on house
2) great exercise → strength & endurance
   - fun way to exercise

 Response

Given the opportunity, I'd like to go rock climbing. One reason is that I've always loved to climb. Although I've never gone rock climbing before, I've spent many afternoons climbing the oak trees in my neighborhood. One time, I even got in trouble for climbing onto the roof on my house. Additionally, I've heard that rock climbing is great exercise because it works out all of a person's major muscle groups. After all, it takes a lot of strength and endurance to pull yourself up the side of a cliff. I'm always looking for fun ways to exercise, and I believe that rock climbing would be both entertaining and physically challenging.

Task 1

Practice 6 — **Your Turn**

Question 1 of 6

Describe a way in which you are different from a friend. What makes your friendship possible in spite of this difference? Use specific reasons and examples to support your answer.

Preparation Time 00:00:15
Response Time 00:00:45

Notes

Opinion: _____

_____

_____

_____

_____

Response

_____

_____

_____

_____

_____

_____

_____

_____

Practice 6 — *Model Answer*

Question 1 of 6

Describe a way in which you are different from a friend. What makes your friendship possible in spite of this difference? Use specific reasons and examples to support your answer.

Notes

Opinion: *Marie = indoors, quiet / me = outdoors, talkative*

1) share interests → watching movies @ home, walking, talking @ coffee shop

2) in-between activities (mall) → compromise

- *½ talk, ½ browse*

 Response

My friend Marie likes to spend time indoors, and she's usually pretty quiet. I'm the opposite, as I usually prefer to go outdoors, and I like talking all the time. We're able to stay friends mainly because each of us likes to do a little bit of what the other likes. So sometimes I enjoy watching a movie indoors with Marie, and sometimes she enjoys going for a walk with me and chatting at a local coffee shop. One more reason is that we can share "in-between" activities such as shopping at the mall. When we're at the mall, we talk about half the time and quietly browse about half the time. So overall, both of us compromise to make our friendship possible.

Task 1

Practice 7 **Your Turn**

Question 1 of 6

Describe an event or series of events from your childhood that have greatly influenced you as an adult. Explain how this event influenced you. Use specific reasons and examples to support your answer.

Preparation Time 00:00:15
Response Time 00:00:45

Notes

Opinion: _____

_____

_____

_____

_____

Response

_____

_____

_____

_____

_____

_____

_____

_____

Task 1

Practice 7 — *Model Answer*

Question 1 of 6

Describe an event or series of events from your childhood that have greatly influenced you as an adult. Explain how this event influenced you. Use specific reasons and examples to support your answer.

Notes

Opinion: _moved a lot_

1) easily adapt to change (new friends/places)
  - most ppl. = change hard

2) cultivated curiosity from moving
  - moving to new place → diff. sights → wonder abt. world → travel

 Response

One aspect of my childhood that has had a big influence on my adult life was the fact that I moved around a lot. First, moving around taught me to adapt to change. By moving so much as a child, I got used to making new friends and finding new places to hang out. Most people have trouble adapting to life in a new place, but I do so very easily. As a result, I've cultivated great curiosity about the world. Whenever I moved to new places, I always found something unique and different there. All this traveling and exploring made me wonder about other places that I've never been to, causing me to want to travel more as an adult.

Task 1

Practice 8 — Your Turn

Question 1 of 6

Many people feel shy in certain circumstances. What helps people overcome shyness, in your experience? Use specific reasons and examples to support your answer.

Preparation Time 00:00:15
Response Time 00:00:45

Notes

Opinion: _____

Response

Practice 8 — Model Answer

Question 1 of 6

Many people feel shy in certain circumstances. What helps people overcome shyness, in your experience? Use specific reasons and examples to support your answer.

Notes

Opinion: _overcome = diff. but possible_

1) Josh, ice-breakers
   - prepare for convo., boost confidence

2) find other shy ppl.
   - introduce, compliment

 Response

In my experience, it's very difficult to overcome shyness, but I've come across a couple of strategies that work well. The first strategy I use is something I learned from my friend, Josh. When my friend Josh feels shy about calling someone or meeting with someone, he writes down a list of "ice-breaker" questions and conversation starters beforehand. Even if he doesn't end up using the ideas he listed, he still feels more confident. The second strategy I've learned is that when you feel shy at a party where there are lots of people, look around and find someone else who seems to feel shy. Then concentrate on making that person feel better by introducing yourself and if possible, giving the person some kind of compliment.

Practice 9 — Your Turn

Question 1 of 6

What is the best gift that you have ever received? Explain what made this gift so unique. Use specific reasons and examples to support your answer.

Preparation Time 00:00:15
Response Time 00:00:45

Notes

Opinion: _____

_____

_____

_____

_____

Response

_____

_____

_____

_____

_____

_____

_____

_____

_____

Task 1

Practice 9 — Model Answer

Question 1 of 6

What is the best gift that you have ever received? Explain what made this gift so unique. Use specific reasons and examples to support your answer.

Notes

Opinion: _puppy_

1) learned responsibility
   - feed, walk, clean, vet. → responsible now
2) my best friend → no sis./bro.
   - when angry → soothing

 Response

By far the best gift I've ever received was a puppy, which I got for a birthday present when I was young. The puppy was the best gift because taking care of her helped me develop a sense of responsibility. For example, after receiving the dog, I had to feed her, walk her, and clean up after her. One time, I even saved up money so I could take my dog to the vet when she became sick. Thanks to these experiences, I now consider myself a very responsible person. Moreover, the puppy became my best friend. Since I have no sisters or brothers, I would've been very lonely without it. Also, I found her presence very soothing whenever I was angry or stressed out. As a result, the dog helped me become a more calm and relaxed person.

Task 1

Practice 10 — **Your Turn**

Question 1 of 6

What is one traditional meal or dish from your home country that you think people should try? Explain why you think people should try this food. Use reasons and details to support your answer.

Preparation Time 00:00:15
Response Time   00:00:45

Notes

Opinion: _____

_____

_____

_____

_____

Response

_____

_____

_____

_____

_____

_____

_____

_____

_____

Task 1

Practice 10 — Model Answer

Question 1 of 6

What is one traditional meal or dish from your home country that you think people should try? Explain why you think people should try this food. Use reasons and details to support your answer.

Notes

Opinion: _kimchi_

1) national food → experience South Korea
   - first weird → delightful
2) health benefits
   - prevent cancer, good for intestines, digestion

 Response

I believe kimchi is one food from my home country of South Korea that people should try. First, kimchi is the national food of South Korea. Therefore, people should try kimchi so they can experience the taste that represents Korea. Although kimchi might taste a little weird at first, once people get used to it, they realize that it has a delightful flavor. Furthermore, kimchi is internationally recognized for its health benefits. For instance, it's now widely believed that eating kimchi reduces a person's risk of developing cancer. Also, it's good for the intestines and digestion. Thus, people should try kimchi not only for its taste, but also for the health benefits.

Now practice saying your response aloud. If possible, have a friend or a classmate fill out this checklist as you say your response to him or her. If you are by yourself, record and listen to your response, and then fill out the checklist below on your own.

Deliver your response within 45 seconds.

Task 1 Response Checklist

	Yes	Somewhat	No
• Does the speaker give his or her opinion in a topic statement?			
• Does the speaker support his or her opinion with at least two details or reasons?			
• Does the speaker support his or her opinion with at least two details or reasons?			
• Does the speaker deliver a coherent response by using appropriate tone and pronunciation?			
• Does the speaker finish within the time limit?			

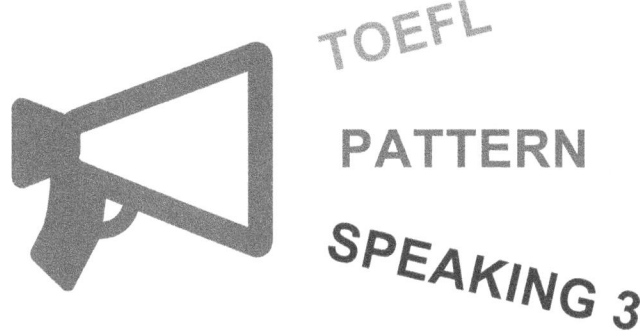

CHAPTER 2

Selecting a Preference

Chapter 2 Selecting a Preference

GENERAL BACKGROUND INFORMATION

1. EXPLANATION OF TASK 2

Speaking Task 2 presents two possible activities, situations, or opinions. Choose which one of the two options you prefer, and then explain your preference with reasons and details. A narrator will read the prompt aloud; the prompt will stay on the computer screen during your preparation and response time.

You will then have 15 seconds to prepare your response. Begin preparing when the "Preparation Time" notice appears on your screen. Use the time to write down a few notes in outline form because you will not have enough time to write a full answer.

At the end of 15 seconds, you will hear a short beep. The "Preparation Time" notice changes to "Response Time." The countdown from 45 seconds begins. Your response will be recorded during the 45 seconds. At the end, the recording will stop. A new screen will indicate that the response time has ended.

2. NECESSARY SKILLS FOR TASK 2

You must be able to:

- take a position and support the position with reasons
- organize ideas coherently with a clear topic statement and supporting reasons
- speak clearly using correct grammar, vocabulary, and pronunciation

3. EXPLANATION OF QUESTION TYPES

The question will always ask that you respond with your preference and give reasons for your response. Your score is not based upon your preference but on how well you explain your preference.

Question Types

1 Picking a Preference about a University Issue

Some students prefer X (first university-related preference). Other students prefer Y (second university-related preference). Which do you prefer and why? Use specific reasons and examples to support your answer.

2 Picking a Lifestyle or Ethical Preference

Some people believe X (first lifestyle/ethical preference). Other people believe Y (second lifestyle/ethical preference). Which opinion do you agree with and why? Use specific details and examples to support your preference.

4. EXAMPLE PROMPTS

Possible Task 2 prompts that you may encounter on the official TOEFL exam include:

> **Prompt**
>
> - Do you agree or disagree with the following statement? Earth is being harmed by human activities. Give reasons and details to support your answer.
>
> - Some people only like to do what they can already do well. Other people like to try new things and take risks. Which do you prefer and why? Use specific reasons and examples to support your answer.
>
> - Some people prefer living where the weather is always the same. Other people prefer living where the weather changes every season. Which do you prefer and why? Support your answer with reasons.
>
> - Some people like to shop online. Some people like to shop in person. Which do you prefer and why? Support your answer with reasons and details.
>
> - Do you agree or disagree with the following statement? The Internet has made it easier and more convenient for people to access accurate information. Use reasons and details to support your answer.

5. USEFUL EXPRESSIONS

Some useful expressions for Task 1 are:

- In my opinion, _____.

- I agree (that) _____ because _____.

- I disagree (that) _____ because _____.

- I prefer _____ to _____ because _____.
  (noun / noun phrase)   (noun / noun phrase)

- I prefer to _____ than to _____ because _____.
  (verb / verb phrase)   (verb / verb phrase)

- I think (that) _____ is better than _____ because _____.

- I believe (that) _____ is preferable to _____ because _____.

- Given the choice between _____ and _____, I prefer _____ because _____.

HACKING STRATEGY

STEP 1. Outline Your Response

- Read the prompt carefully
- Decide on a preference

STEP 2. Prepare Your Response

- Make your opinion into a topic statement
- Add reasons that support your preference

STEP 3. Deliver Your Response

- Respond using coherent sentences
- Add transition words between ideas

EXAMPLE 1

STEP 1. OUTLINE YOUR RESPONSE

As you read and listen to the prompt, start outlining a response that includes two details or examples that support your preference.

> **Prompt**
> Some people prefer to live in a small town. Others prefer to live in a big city. Which place would you prefer to live in? Use specific reasons and examples to support your answer.

First, decide on a preference that you feel you can talk about for 45 seconds.

- **Preference:** *big city*

STEP 2. PREPARE YOUR RESPONSE

When organizing your response, you should make your preference into a topic statement and come up with at least two reasons or details that support your topic statement. Because you are only given 15 seconds to prepare for your response, you must organize your thoughts quickly.

- **Topic Statement:** *While some people prefer to live in a small town, I prefer to live in a big city.*
  - **Reason 1:** *more activities: movies, shop / + restaurants*
  - **Reason 2:** *meet more people: single / friends, dating*

STEP 3. DELIVER YOUR RESPONSE

Use the outline that you created in STEP 2 to guide you as you deliver your response. Respond using complete sentences, and add transition words to show how ideas relate to one another.

> *While some people prefer to live in a small town, I prefer to live in a big city.* **First**, *there are more activities in a big city.* **For example**, *being in a big city gives me plenty of opportunities to see movies and go shopping.* **Moreover**, *big cities have many restaurants where I can try new dishes. In a small town, there are not many places to visit.* **Also**, *there are more people to meet in big cities. I'm young and single, and I'm interested in making new friends and dating. Ultimately, I'd definitely prefer to live in a big city than in a small town.*

EXAMPLE 2

STEP 1. OUTLINE YOUR RESPONSE

As you read and listen to the prompt, start outlining a response that includes two details or examples that support your preference.

> **Prompt**
> Do you agree or disagree with the following statement? Childhood is the most important stage of a person's life. Use specific reasons and examples to support your answer.

First, decide on a preference that you feel you can talk about for 45 seconds.

- Preference: *disagree*

STEP 2. PREPARE YOUR RESPONSE

When organizing your response, you should make your preference into a topic statement and come up with at least two reasons or details that support your topic statement. Because you are only given 15 seconds to prepare for your response, you must organize your thoughts quickly.

- Topic Statement: *I disagree with the statement that childhood is the most important time in one's life.*
    - Reason 1: *childhood → determine personality: good or bad*
    - Reason 2: *adult → willpower: no matter how diff. / change situation or attitude*

STEP 3. DELIVER YOUR RESPONSE

Use the outline that you created in STEP 2 to guide you as you deliver your response. Respond using complete sentences, and add transition words to show how ideas relate to one another.

> *I disagree with the statement that childhood is the most important time in one's life.* **Of course**, *childhood is still an important stage in one's life. During this time, many features of one's personality develop. Based on a person's childhood, he or she can develop into a positive and happy person, or a negative and bitter person later in life.* **However**, *as children grow up and become adults, they develop a very important trait called willpower. Because of willpower, one can overcome any obstacles they faced during childhood by believing that they have the power to change as adults. Willpower allows one to overcome their own past. So, as far as I'm concerned, childhood is not nearly as important as adulthood.*

Task 2

Practice 1  **Your Turn**

Question 2 of 6

Some people enjoy cooking while others consider it a chore. Which viewpoint do you hold and why? Use specific reasons and examples to support your answer.

 Preparation Time 00:00:15
Response Time 00:00:45

Notes

Preference: _____

_____

_____

_____

_____

Response

Task 2

Practice 1 — Model Answer

Question 2 of 6

Some people enjoy cooking while others consider it a chore. Which viewpoint do you hold and why? Use specific reasons and examples to support your answer.

Notes

Preference: _cooking = chore_

1) requires planning → shop for ingredients
   - prefer spontaneous → restaurant

2) dislike washing dishes
   - restaurant → avoid planning, dishes

 Response

It's understandable that some people consider cooking to be fun, but for me it's more of a chore. For one, cooking requires at least a minimum of planning because you have to shop for the ingredients ahead of time. I like to be more spontaneous and just go out to a restaurant and order whatever I feel like eating at the moment. A second reason I don't like cooking is that I don't like washing dishes because it always seems to take a long time. In my opinion, it's worthwhile to spend a little more money to eat out and avoid planning ahead and washing dishes.

Task 2

Practice 2 — Your Turn

Question 2 of 6

Some movies encourage audiences to think about serious issues. Other movies amuse and entertain audiences. Which type of movie do you prefer? Use reasons and examples to support your answer.

Preparation Time 00:00:15
Response Time   00:00:45

Notes

Preference: _____

_____

_____

_____

_____

Response

_____

_____

_____

_____

_____

_____

_____

_____

_____

_____

Task 2

Practice 2 — Model Answer

Question 2 of 6

Some movies encourage audiences to think about serious issues. Other movies amuse and entertain audiences. Which type of movie do you prefer? Use reasons and examples to support your answer.

Notes

Preference: *serious*

1) plots → more complex
   - holds my attention
   - funny movies → simple & easily bored of
2) learn → dramatize events

 Response

While some people like movies that are fun and entertaining, I prefer movies that are serious and thought-provoking. First, I prefer serious movies because of their complex plots. These complex plots hold my attention, keeping me interested in the characters and their stories. But funny movies usually depict simple characters and predicable stories, causing me to become bored quickly. Additionally, I like serious movies because I can always learn something from them. For example, serious movies often dramatize current or historical events, causing me to think about social issues such as equality and the meaning of justice.

Task 2

Practice 3 — Your Turn

Question 2 of 6

Your school has enough money to purchase computers for students or books for the library. Which of these choices would you recommend? Support your answer with specific reasons and examples.

Preparation Time 00:00:15
Response Time 00:00:45

Notes

Preference: _____

_____

_____

_____

_____

Response

_____

_____

_____

_____

_____

_____

_____

_____

_____

Task 2

Practice 3 — *Model Answer*

Question 2 of 6

Your school has enough money to purchase computers for students or books for the library. Which of these choices would you recommend? Support your answer with specific reasons and examples.

Notes

Preference: _books_

1) most already have latest comp. → waste of money

2) few, outdated
   - only have old
   - quality info.

 Response

Given enough money to buy either computers or books, I believe the school should invest in new books for the library. First, most students at my school already own the latest computers, so it'd be a waste of money for the school to spend money providing students with something they already have. Second, there are very few books in our library, and all of them are outdated. All of the books in our library were written at least 10 years ago. Although the students can access a lot of information using computers, they still need various reference books, textbooks, and primary sources to find quality information.

Task 2

Practice 4 — Your Turn

Question 2 of 6

Some people prefer to save the money that they earn for the future, while others prefer to spend money on activities that they enjoy doing. Which do you prefer and why? Use specific reasons in your answer.

Preparation Time 00:00:15
Response Time 00:00:45

Notes

Preference: _____

_____

_____

_____

_____

Response

_____

_____

_____

_____

_____

_____

_____

_____

_____

_____

Practice 4 — Model Answer

Question 2 of 6

Some people prefer to save the money that they earn for the future, while others prefer to spend money on activities that they enjoy doing. Which do you prefer and why? Use specific reasons in your answer.

Notes

Preference: _save $_

1) good for present
  - no $ worries = no anxious
  - can afford time off

2) good for future → retirement, vacation fund

 Response

When I get a paycheck from my work, I try to save as much money as possible. I believe that doing so will make me happier now and in my future. First, I believe that saving money allows me to enjoy the present. Because I always have money in my savings account, I never have to worry about being able to pay for rent or car insurance. Thus, my savings account reduces my anxiety. Additionally, saving money allows me to take a day or two off work if I'm sick or just need some time to relax. Moreover, saving money allows me to prepare for my future. Every month, I put some of my paycheck toward a retirement fund. Doing so ensures that I don't have to work for the rest of my life. I also put some of my savings in a vacation fund. That way, once a year, I can take time off work and go on a long, exciting vacation.

Task 2

Practice 5  **Your Turn**

Question 2 of 6

Do you agree or disagree with the following statement? Using social media is a valuable pastime. Use specific reasons and details to support your answer.

 Preparation Time 00:00:15
Response Time 00:00:45

Notes

Preference: _____

_____

_____

_____

_____

Response

_____

_____

_____

_____

_____

_____

_____

_____

_____

Task 2

Practice 5 — Model Answer

Question 2 of 6

Do you agree or disagree with the following statement? Using social media is a valuable pastime. Use specific reasons and details to support your answer.

Notes

Preference: _agree_

1) creativity, humor
   - share funny ideas, pics, vids
   - reminded of friends
2) find support, comfort

 Response

I agree that using social media is a valuable pastime because doing so is often uplifting. In my experience, social media brings out creativity and humor in people, and they entertain each other by sharing thoughts, pictures, or videos, such as funny antics of cats or dogs. As a result, I often find myself smiling when I go on social media because doing so reminds me of how much I like my friends. Of course, life isn't always happy, and the few times I've shared information about difficulties I was facing, many people near and far responded with supportive comments. So for me, social media is valuable because it gives me positive feelings.

Task 2

Practice 6   **Your Turn**

Question 2 of 6

Do you agree or disagree with the following statement? The use of automobiles has improved modern life. Use specific reasons and details to support your answer.

Preparation Time   00:00:15
Response Time   00:00:45

Notes

Preference: _____

_____

_____

_____

_____

Response

Task 2

Practice 6 — Model Answer

Question 2 of 6

Do you agree or disagree with the following statement? The use of automobiles has improved modern life. Use specific reasons and details to support your answer.

Notes

Preference: _agree_

1) comfort, ease

2) time save

- past → 1) horse, foot   2) days/weeks
- now → 1) padded, climate   2) hrs.

Response

While some people think automobiles cause too many problems, I think they've improved far more lives than they've harmed. For one thing, the use of automobiles has made travel much more comfortable and convenient. In the past, people traveled by horse or on foot in uncomfortable and even unsafe conditions. Now, people can travel by automobile in comfortable seats and climate-controlled conditions. Moreover, automobiles have saved us a lot of time. In the past, people spent days or weeks traveling relatively short distances. These days, a person can travel hundreds of kilometers in a matter of hours by automobile.

Task 2

Practice 7   **Your Turn**

Question 2 of 6

Some people like to eat their meals with their friends or family members. Other people like to eat alone. Which do you prefer and why? Support your answer with reasons.

Preparation Time 00:00:15
Response Time 00:00:45

Notes

Preference: _____

_____

_____

_____

_____

Response

Task 2

Practice 7 — Model Answer

Question 2 of 6

Some people like to eat their meals with their friends or family members. Other people like to eat alone. Which do you prefer and why? Support your answer with reasons.

Notes

Preference: _fam./friends_

1) fam., good relationship

　· dinner → share story → helps bond

2) friends, stress ↓

　· prob. → advice

 Response

Although there may be some benefits to eating alone, I prefer to eat my meals with family members and friends for a couple of reasons. First, I think eating with members of my family helps me build good relationships with them. For example, during dinner, family members may share stories about what they did during the day. These stories and conversations help my family understand one another and strengthen family ties. Also, eating with friends helps relieve my stress. For example, when I eat dinner with my friends, I can talk about my problems and ask for their advice. This always makes me feel much better, and I always feel less anxious after these meals.

Task 2

Practice 8 — Your Turn

Question 2 of 6

Some people like to take vacations in a big, busy city. Other people like to take vacations in a quiet, rural countryside. Which do you prefer and why? Support your answer with reasons.

Preparation Time 00:00:15
Response Time 00:00:45

Notes

Preference: _____

Response

Task 2

Practice 8 — Model Answer

Question 2 of 6

Some people like to take vacations in a big, busy city. Other people like to take vacations in a quiet, rural countryside. Which do you prefer and why? Support your answer with reasons.

Notes

Preference: *big city*

1) many sites

- *Paris → Eiffel, Louvre, Versailles*

2) many new ppl.

- *how diff. culture think, talk, act*

 Response

Whenever I go on vacation, I prefer to spend my time in a big, bustling city for a number of reasons. First, most cities have many exciting cultural sites to see. In fact, one of my wishes is to visit Paris because of its magnificent sightseeing attractions. I want to visit the Eiffel tower, the Louvre museum, and the Palace of Versailles, as all of these impressive sights are filled with interesting history. Also, I like meeting many new people during my vacations. During a trip to a big city, I can meet lots of people from different countries. By getting to know these people, I get many opportunities to see how other people from different cultures think, talk, and act.

Task 2
Practice 9 — Your Turn

Question 2 of 6

Some teachers prefer to grade their students based on one long final exam. Other teachers prefer to grade their students based on several shorter tests given throughout the course. Which grading method do you prefer? Support you answer with reasons and details.

Preparation Time 00:00:15
Response Time   00:00:45

Notes

Preference: _____

_____
_____
_____
_____

Response

Task 2

Practice 9 — Model Answer

Question 2 of 6

Some teachers prefer to grade their students based on one long final exam. Other teachers prefer to grade their students based on several shorter tests given throughout the course. Which grading method do you prefer? Support you answer with reasons and details.

Notes

Preference: *one long exam (LE)*

1) *way of studying*

2) *lvl. of difficulty*

- *several SEs → 1) just memorize w/o understanding   2) hard, limited*
- *one LE → 1) understand all info.   2) easy*

Response

In a class, I prefer to be graded based on the results of one long exam than based on the results of several short exams. First, when taking several short exams, many students tend to memorize the materials without even understanding them. Conversely, to do well on one long exam, students have to listen to every lecture and make sure they understand all the information at the end of the course. Also, when taking several short exams, the questions are usually difficult and specific because the test material is very limited. However, I don't think this is a good way of testing students. With one long exam, I believe that students are graded on whether they understand the most important overall concepts rather than the minor details.

Task 2

Practice 10 — Your Turn

Question 2 of 6

When under a lot of stress, some people prefer to stay home while others prefer to go out. Which do you prefer and why? Support your answer with specific reasons and details.

Preparation Time 00:00:15
Response Time 00:00:45

Notes

Preference: _____

_____

_____

_____

_____

Response

Task 2

Practice 10 — Model Answer

Question 2 of 6

When under a lot of stress, some people prefer to stay home while others prefer to go out. Which do you prefer and why? Support your answer with specific reasons and details.

Notes

Preference: _go out_

1) home → boring
   - comfortable, but not much to do (sleep, TV, Internet)

2) outside → clear head, relieve stress from studying
   - downtown, look around, people-watch

 Response

While some people want to stay home when they are stressed, I prefer to go out to relieve stress. For one thing, I often find that staying in my house is too boring. Of course, staying at home is often very comfortable, but I usually find that there're not many things to do at home except sleep, watch TV, or surf the Internet. However, if I go outside, I feel good because I can clear my head. Since most of my stress comes from studying too hard, I really need to take a break from time to time. I don't need to go anywhere special, though. Just walking downtown, looking around, people-watching help me relieve my stress.

Now practice saying your response aloud. If possible, have a friend/classmate fill out this checklist as you say your response to him or her. If you are by yourself, record and listen to your response, and then fill out the checklist below on your own.

Deliver your response within 45 seconds.

Task 2 Response Checklist

	Yes	Somewhat	No
• Does the speaker give his or her opinion in a topic statement?			
• Does the speaker support his or her preference with at least two details or reasons?			
• Does the speaker deliver an organized response by using transition words and proper sentence structures?			
• Does the speaker deliver a coherent response by using appropriate tone and pronunciation?			
• Does the speaker finish within the time limit?			

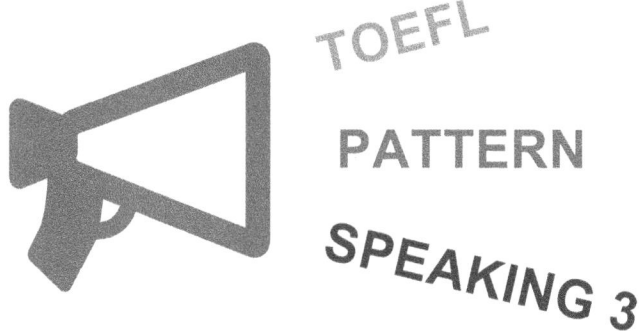

CHAPTER 3

Campus Situation
(Reading and Listening)

Chapter 3

Campus Situation

GENERAL BACKGROUND INFORMATION

1. EXPLANATION OF TASK 3

Speaking Task 3 requires that you read a brief announcement of 75 to 100 words about a change on campus; the announcement may be presented in the form of a newspaper article or a campus-wide notification. You will be given 45 to 50 seconds to read the announcement. Common topics include:

- building, updating, or improving structures on campus
- creating and enforcing new campus rules and regulations
- changing admission, registration, or graduation requirements

The announcement presents information about a proposed change to campus, including two or more reasons for this change.

After reading the announcement, you will listen to two students discuss the subject presented in the announcement. One speaker will either strongly support or oppose the change. The conversation is 60 to 80 seconds long.

After the conversation ends, you will be given a prompt related to what you have read and heard. The prompt appears on your computer screen and is read aloud by a narrator.

> **Prompt**
>
> The man/woman expresses his/her opinion about the plan described in the announcement. Briefly summarize the plan. Then state his/her opinion about the plan and explain the reasons he/she gives for holding that opinion.

After seeing the prompt, you have 30 seconds of "Preparation Time" to prepare your response. At the end, you will hear a short beep. The clock then changes to "Response Time" and begins to count down.

You have 60 seconds to respond. At the end of the 60 seconds, the recording ends and a new message alerts you that the response time is over.

You may take notes while reading, listening, and preparing. You also may check your notes when responding to the question.

2. NECESSARY SKILLS FOR TASK 3

You must be able to:

- understand information from written and spoken sources regarding campus-based subject matter
- identify and summarize major points and important details from written and spoken sources
- synthesize information from written and spoken sources

HACKING STRATEGY

STEP 1. OUTLINE YOUR RESPONSE

- Take notes as you read the announcement
- Take notes as you listen to the conversation
- Read the prompt carefully

STEP 2. PREPARE YOUR RESPONSE

- Summarize the university's announcement
- State the student's opinion regarding the announcement
- State the student's reasons for holding this opinion

STEP 3. DELIVER YOUR RESPONSE

- Respond using coherent sentences
- Add transition words between ideas

HACKING STRATEGY EXAMPLE

STEP 1. OUTLINE YOUR RESPONSE

Take notes on essential information as you read the university's announcement and listen to the conversation. Do not take notes using full sentences, as you will not have time to do so.

UNIVERSITY ANNOUNCEMENT

Jones University to Change Admission Requirements

Jones Universtiy will begin administering its own math and writing tests to all new students starting next year. These two tests will be given in addition to the traditional SAT test. The new tests will be designed to "screen out" students not yet prepared for math and writing at the university level. While some students may consider the additional tests an inconvenience, the university administration feels that these tests are better than having students fail several classes during their first year. The number of "F's" given in first year classes has risen dramatically over the past five years. Hopefully, this program will remedy this issue.

ANNOUNCEMENT NOTES

new admission requirement (math & writing tests + SAT)

CONVERSATION

F: *Do you believe this? The university is actually going to make its admission requirements harder!*

M: *Oh, yeah, I definitely read about that. It sounds like a lot of new students are having trouble with their introductory classes.*

F: *Well, you'd think so from reading the article. But I think what the university is proposing is a really bad idea. For one, I don't think that the new students' failing their first year classes has much to do with ability. Have you noticed how much the partying has increased on campus since we were freshmen four years ago? Sometimes, it seems like all these new students do is party and hang out at the beach all day.*

M: *You know, now that you mention it, I've noticed that. I mean, my grades suffered a bit as a freshman due to my partying. But I still think all these new students have to have the basic skills to at least pass their first-year classes.*

F: *Right. But all students do have the "basic" skills to perform in these classes. I mean, if their grades were good in high school and they did well on the SAT, they must have some rudimentary skills, right? Plus, people shouldn't have to be complete experts in math and writing before they enter the university. I mean, there should be some room for them to learn.*

F: Female Student / **M:** Male Student

CONVERSATION NOTES

woman opposes
1) failing classes → not ability
  • partying
  • not studying → real cause

2) f-men have basic skills
  • good in HS, SAT OK
  • can't be experts

Once you have taken notes on the announcement and the conversation, carefully read the prompt.

> **Prompt**
>
> The woman expresses her opinion about the plan described in the announcement. Briefly summarize the plan. Then state her opinion about the plan and explain the reasons she gives for holding that opinion.

STEP 2. PREPARE YOUR RESPONSE

During the 30-second preparation time, make sure that your notes address all the points in the prompt, and use the information in your notes to organize your response. Because you only have 30 seconds to prepare your response, do not write using complete sentences.

1) Make sure that you can summarize the university's proposal.
   From Notes → Proposal: *new admission requirement (math and writing tests + SAT)*

2) Make sure that you know whether the speaker supports or opposes the proposal.
   From Notes → Speaker's opinion: *woman opposes*

3) Make sure that you know why the student either supports or opposes the proposal.
   From Notes → Reason 1: *not studying → real reason students fail*
   → Reason 2: *freshmen already have basic skills necessary for university*

STEP 3. DELIVER YOUR RESPONSE

Use the outline that you created in STEP 2 to guide you as you deliver your response. Respond using complete sentences, and add transition words to show how ideas relate to one another.

The university announced that it'll require all new students to take math and writing tests as well as the SAT to fulfill admissions requirements. **The woman believes that the proposal is** *a bad idea.* **To start, the woman questions** *the university's assumption that most new students lack the academic ability to pass their classes.* **She points out that** *a larger number of new students have been partying instead of studying.* **She thinks** *this lack of academic commitment, and not lack of ability, may be the real cause of the new students' bad grades.* **Second, she argues that** *most of the students entering the university already have basic academic skills. They have proven these skills by getting good grades in high school and doing well on the SAT. She says that for those students, it's normal to have some lack of skill.*

Task 3
Practice 1

Question 3 of 6

 Reading Time 00:00:45

University to Change Schedule

The university will change its schedule next year. Instead of starting in the first week of September, the academic year will begin one month earlier, during the first week of August. The school year will now end in late May instead of late June. This move will save the university thousands of dollars in air conditioning costs, as June is the hottest month of the year. It will also allow the university to get better prices on construction projects, which are lower in June.

Announcement Notes

Proposal: _____

Reasons: _____

Now listen to two students as they discuss the announcement.

Question 3 of 6

Task 3
Your Turn

Conversation Notes

Speaker's opinion: _____

Reason 1: _____
_____

Reason 2: _____
_____

Question 3 of 6

The female student expresses her opinion regarding the announcement. Briefly summarize the announcement. Then state her opinion. Explain the reasons she gives for holding her opinion.

Preparation Time 00:00:30
Response Time   00:01:00

Response

_____
_____
_____
_____
_____
_____
_____
_____

Task 3

Practice 1

Question 3 of 6

 Reading Time 00:00:45

University to Change Schedule

The university will change its schedule next year. Instead of starting in the first week of September, the academic year will begin one month earlier, during the first week of August. The school year will now end in late May instead of late June. This move will save the university thousands of dollars in air conditioning costs, as June is the hottest month of the year. It will also allow the university to get better prices on construction projects, which are lower in June.

Announcement Notes

Proposal: _univ. schedule change → start and end one month earlier_

Reasons: _1) save $ 2) better prices on construction projects_

Now listen to two students as they discuss the announcement.

F: How ridiculous is this school? It's like they don't even care about the students.

M: I assume you're talking about the schedule change for next year? I totally agree. It's absurd. What an inconvenience!

F: I mean, first of all, the schedule change will ruin students' summer plans. My family always goes on vacation in August. And that's the best time to go to the beach, too!

M: Yeah, my family always travels then, too. Looks like I'll be missing out on my vacation this year.

F: I could understand if the school's schedule was being changed to help the students. But to save money? I mean... saving air conditioning and construction costs could be important... but isn't the goal of any university to help students in their studies? It's like the university cares more about the money than its students.

M: Totally. The school needs to get its priorities straight.

F: Female Student / M: Male Student

Task 3
Model Answer

Conversation Notes

Speaker's opinion: _woman opposes_

Reason 1: _1) sched. change = inconvenient → vacation w/ fam. Aug_
- _student summer plans_

Reason 2: _2) not to benefit students, for money → selfish_
- _air condition, construction = priority_

Question 3 of 6

The female student expresses her opinion regarding the announcement. Briefly summarize the announcement. Then state her opinion. Explain the reasons she gives for holding her opinion.

 Response

The university will change its schedule so that school begins and ends one month earlier than in previous years. The woman is opposed to the university's schedule change. First, she opposes this decision because she wants to keep the original schedule. The woman says that she always goes on a vacation with her family in August. She feels that this schedule change will ruin many students' summer plans. The second reason that she doesn't like this decision is because she feels that the school only cares about money, not students. She claims that the school is only thinking about the money it can save by changing the schedule. She argues that students should be the priority, not some air conditioning and construction costs.

Task 3
Practice 2

Question 3 of 6

⏱ Reading Time 00:00:45

University to Change Financial Aid Program Next Year

State University will change its financial aid program next year. Only students who live in university housing will be able to obtain scholarships for the next five years. Students who live with their parents will be able to take out loans, but these students will not receive scholarships. Currently, the school is facing a budget crisis, so it cannot afford to give financial aid to everyone. Additionally, students living with their parents already save thousands of dollars on rent, food, and other costs each year.

Announcement Notes

Proposal: _____

Reasons: _____

Now listen to two students speak about the article.

Question 3 of 6

Task 3
Your Turn

Conversation Notes

Speaker's opinion: _____

Reason 1: _____

_____

Reason 2: _____

_____

Question 3 of 6

The male student expresses his opinion regarding the announcement. Summarize the university's proposal, state his opinion, and explain the reasons he gives for holding that opinion.

Preparation Time 00:00:30
Response Time 00:01:00

Response

_____
_____
_____
_____
_____
_____
_____
_____

Task 3

Practice 2

Question 3 of 6

Reading Time 00:00:45

University to Change Financial Aid Program Next Year

State University will change its financial aid program next year. Only students who live in university housing will be able to obtain scholarships for the next five years. Students who live with their parents will be able to take out loans, but these students will not receive scholarships. Currently, the school is facing a budget crisis, so it cannot afford to give financial aid to everyone. Additionally, students living with their parents already save thousands of dollars on rent, food, and other costs each year.

Announcement Notes

Proposal: change fin. aid program → only for students living on campus

Reasons: 1) budget crisis   2) stu. living w/ parents → already save $

Now listen to two students speak about the article.

M: Wow, this new financial aid policy is terrible.
F: Really? How so? It kind of makes sense to me.
M: Well, just because some students live with their parents, it doesn't mean they need less financial aid. In fact, it often means they need more.
F: What do you mean? It seems like they save money by living at home, right?
M: On the surface, you'd assume that. But in my case, I lived at home because my parents were too poor to afford anything else. In fact, many of my friends were in the same boat as me during their first couple of years here.
F: Oh, I didn't know that. That's really sad.
M: Also, this plan won't really solve the university's budget problem. I mean, most of the kids at this school come from wealthy families. It's only a small percentage of people that really need the scholarships. How can denying 50 people scholarships make up for a 50 million dollar deficit? It doesn't make sense.
F: Right, I see what you're saying. Maybe this proposal isn't such a great idea.
M: They're just driving away the smart but poor students who would otherwise come here to study.

M: Male Student / F: Female Student

Task 3
Model Answer

Conversation Notes

Speaker's opinion: _man opposes_

Reason 1: _(1) stu. live w/ parent → need more $_

▪ too poor to afford other housing

Reason 2: _(2) not solve budget prob. → denying 50 not solve $50 million_

▪ drive away smart/poor

Question 3 of 6

The male student expresses his opinion regarding the announcement. Summarize the university's proposal, state his opinion, and explain the reasons he gives for holding that opinion.

 Response

The man opposes the university's plan to change the financial aid program because it'll no longer accommodate students who are living at home. First, he says that the proposal is unfair to some poor students. He points out that the students living with their parents do so because they can't afford to live anywhere else, so these students likely require more financial aid than students who live on campus. Also, he claims this policy won't solve the university's budget crisis because so few students live at home. Denying 50 people financial help wouldn't solve the multi-million dollar budget problem. In fact, he's sure that the university will just end up losing the smart but poor students who will no longer be able to afford the university's tuition.

Task 3

Practice 3

Question 3 of 6

 Reading Time 00:00:45

University to Change Class Requirements Next Year

State University will change its class requirements next year. All students will be required to enroll in a one-year art series; students will be able to choose from a music, dance, painting, or acting series. The reasons for this are twofold: first, a new study shows students who take art classes are happier and perform better in all their studies. Second, the university president wants to balance out the image of the university as a "hard science" school by making the students more rounded in their studies.

Announcement Notes

Proposal: _____

Reasons: _____

Now listen to two students speak about the article.

Question 3 of 6

Task 3
Your Turn

Conversation Notes

Speaker's opinion: _____

Reason 1: _____

_____

Reason 2: _____

_____

Question 3 of 6

The female student expresses her opinion regarding the announcement. Briefly summarize the announcement. Then state her opinion and explain the reasons she gives for holding her opinion.

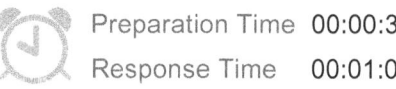

Preparation Time 00:00:30
Response Time   00:01:00

Response

_____
_____
_____
_____
_____
_____
_____
_____

Task 3

Practice 3

Question 3 of 6

⏲ Reading Time 00:00:45

University to Change Class Requirements Next Year

State University will change its class requirements next year. All students will be required to enroll in a one-year art series; students will be able to choose from a music, dance, painting, or acting series. The reasons for this are twofold: first, a new study shows students who take art classes are happier and perform better in all their studies. Second, the university president wants to balance out the image of the university as a "hard science" school by making the students more rounded in their studies.

Announcement Notes

Proposal: _change class requirements one yr. arts series_

Reasons: _1) taking art classes → happier & better_   _2) change univ. image_

Now listen to two students speak about the article.

M: Did you read the article in the school's newspaper about the new class requirement?
F: I did, and I think it's a ridiculous proposal. Why do a couple of chemistry majors like us have to take a year of pointless art classes?
M: Yeah, I've never really been interested in the arts.
F: Forcing us to take these classes won't make students happier, and I guarantee you that it won't make us perform better in our studies, either. I think we'll just have less time to study the subjects that are actually important to us.
M: You can say that again.
F: And you know what really gets me? The university's president almost seems ashamed of our school's reputation as a science school. I mean, I think he should be proud; not every school has students that perform so well in science.
M: I think so, too. He should consider himself lucky.
F: Yeah, he should encourage us to pursue our science education.

M: Male Student / F: Female Student

Task 3
Model Answer

Conversation Notes

Speaker's opinion: *woman opposes*

Reason 1: *not interested in art. forcing → sad, not happy*

↓ student performance, waste time

Reason 2: *Presi. ashamed*

good in sci., lucky → encourage., not discourage

Question 3 of 6

The female student expresses her opinion regarding the announcement. Briefly summarize the announcement. Then state her opinion and explain the reasons she gives for holding her opinion.

 Response

The woman dislikes the university's decision concerning new class requirements that will make all students take a year of art classes. First, she feels unhappy about the change because she's not interested in arts. She believes that forcing students to study a subject that they don't care about will make them angry, not happy. She also argues that this policy won't encourage students to perform better. Instead, she feels that it'll distract students from subjects they're passionate about. Second, she's disappointed by the president's attitude. She thinks that the president should feel lucky about the students' excellence in science and should encourage students to pursue their passion, not discourage them.

Task 3

Practice 4

Question 3 of 6

 Reading Time 00:00:45

Announcement from the President

The university administration believes that it is time to rebuild the old campus theater. The new theater would be four times as large as the current theater. It would have comfortable seating, a super-sized screen for movies, and the latest sound system for concerts and performances. The current campus theater, one of the oldest buildings on campus, was built when the university was founded in the 1920s. At that time, the student population was less than 1,000, and the only performances offered on campus were dramatic plays. Today, there is a student body of over 20,000, and the theater hosts weekly movies, concerts, and other live performances.

Announcement Notes

Proposal: _____

Reasons: _____

Now listen to two students as they discuss the announcement.

Question 3 of 6

Task 3
Your Turn

Conversation Notes

Speaker's opinion: _____

Reason 1: _____

_____

Reason 2: _____

_____

Question 3 of 6

The female student expresses her opinion regarding the announcement. Briefly summarize the announcement. Then state her opinion and the reasons she gives for holding her opinion.

Preparation Time 00:00:30
Response Time 00:01:00

Response

_____
_____
_____
_____
_____
_____
_____
_____

Task 3

Practice 4

Question 3 of 6

Reading Time 00:00:45

Announcement from the President

The university administration believes that it is time to rebuild the old campus theater. The new theater would be four times as large as the current theater. It would have comfortable seating, a super-sized screen for movies, and the latest sound system for concerts and performances. The current campus theater, one of the oldest buildings on campus, was built when the university was founded in the 1920s. At that time, the student population was less than 1,000, and the only performances offered on campus were dramatic plays. Today, there is a student body of over 20,000, and the theater hosts weekly movies, concerts, and other live performances.

Announcement Notes

Proposal: _rebuild campus theater_

Reasons: _more students now than when it was built_

Now listen to two students as they discuss the announcement.

M: Wow, did you read that the university plans to rebuild the old campus theater? It's pretty exciting, isn't it?

F: Really, do you think so? Well, I couldn't disagree more.

M: Why do you say that?

F: Well, for one thing, I couldn't care less about seeing movies, concerts, or other big performances on campus. I mean, there's a brand-new movie theater that's just a ten-minute walk from campus. And there are plenty of great venues downtown for concerts.

M: That's true. But wouldn't it be more convenient for us to see all those things right here on campus?

F: Well, maybe. But in addition to movies and concerts, downtown has a lot more things to do, like bowling and billiards.

M: Yeah, I understand what you're saying.

F: And anyway, I love the old theater building! I mean, the 1920s architecture is beautiful and rare. I can't believe that the university would even consider destroying such a historic building.

M: Wow, I didn't even think about that.

M: Male Student / F: Female Student

Task 3
Model Answer

Conversation Notes

Speaker's opinion: _woman opposes_

Reason 1: _new → not necessary; movie near, concert downtown_

　　　　　· _downtown, more to do → bowling, billiards_

Reason 2: _love old theater → arch. beautiful & rare_

　　　　　· _destroying hist. → bad_

Question 3 of 6

The female student expresses her opinion regarding the announcement. Briefly summarize the announcement. Then state her opinion and the reasons she gives for holding her opinion.

 Response

The woman is opposed to the university's plan to tear down the old campus theater and build a new one for a couple of reasons. First of all, she doesn't care about seeing movies and other shows on campus. She says that there's a new movie theater within walking distance of campus, and she can attend concerts in any number of venues downtown. She also says that downtown offers other fun activities such as bowling and billiards. In addition, she loves the old theater building the way it is and wants the school to preserve it. She thinks that the architecture is beautiful and unique. Therefore, she doesn't understand why the university wants to destroy such a historic building.

Task 3

Practice 5

Question 3 of 6

⏱ Reading Time 00:00:45

University to Start Electronic Registration Next Semester

Next semester, the university will finally implement its long-awaited electronic registration system. The system will do away with long lines, waits, and hassles at the university registrar's office. Once the system is in place, students will no longer register for classes using the paper-based method currently in use at the registrar's office. Instead, students will register through the Internet using our electronic system. The system is quick, efficient, and easy to use. Confirmation of class registration can be printed from the computer or sent as an email. Best of all, the system will be free for all students to use. Students will be able to see how many empty spots ther are in the classes that they want to register for at home.

Announcement Notes

Proposal: _____

Reasons: _____

Now listen to two students as they discuss the announcement.

Question 3 of 6

Task 3
Your Turn

Conversation Notes

Speaker's opinion: _____

Reason 1: _____
_____

Reason 2: _____
_____

Question 3 of 6

The woman expresses her opinion of the new electronic registration system. Briefly summarize the announcement. Then state her opinion and state the reasons she gives for holding her opinion.

 Preparation Time 00:00:30
Response Time 00:01:00

Response

_____
_____
_____
_____
_____
_____
_____
_____

Task 3

Practice 5

Question 3 of 6

Reading Time 00:00:45

University to Start Electronic Registration Next Semester

Next semester, the university will finally implement its long-awaited electronic registration system. The system will do away with long lines, waits, and hassles at the university registrar's office. Once the system is in place, students will no longer register for classes using the paper-based method currently in use at the registrar's office. Instead, students will register through the Internet using our electronic system. The system is quick, efficient, and easy to use. Confirmation of class registration can be printed from the computer or sent as an email. Best of all, the system will be free for all students to use. Students will be able to see how many empty spots ther are in the classes that they want to register for at home.

Announcement Notes

Proposal: _ppr.-based reg. → comp. based reg._

Reasons: _1) quick, efficient, easy to use, free_   _2) register from home_

Now listen to two students as they discuss the announcement.

M: I'm glad we're finally getting this electronic class registration system, aren't you?

F: Yeah, I think this system will work way better. I mean, I think we're just about the only university that doesn't have a computer registration system yet.

M: I guess that's probably true. Our university will finally be joining the 21st century.
(Both laugh)

F: With the computer registration system, it'll be way easier to make changes to our schedules. I mean, with the current system, we have to have our professors fill out a form whenever we want to drop or add a class. But with the new system, dropping a class or adding a new one really will be as easy as clicking a button.

M: That's true. I hadn't even considered that.

F: And the announcement says that we can get our confirmation sent to us by email instead of paper confirmation. I'm pretty disorganized, so receiving an email confirmation is way better than all those paper confirmations. I just end up losing all of them anyway.

M: I'm right with you there. I don't know of anyone who keeps track of the paper confirmations we get now.

F: And anyway, receiving the class signup confirmations by email will save a lot of paper.

M: Good point.

M: Male Student / F: Female Student

Task 3

...Model Answer

Conversation Notes

Speaker's opinion: _woman supports_

Reason 1: _easier to change sched._
 • _no forms for prof. to sign_

Reason 2: _convenient confirmation_
 • _ppr. confirm. = easy to lose / email confirm. = good for env._

Question 3 of 6

The woman expresses her opinion of the new electronic registration system. Briefly summarize the announcement. Then state her opinion and state the reasons she gives for holding her opinion.

 Response

The woman is in favor of the new computer-based class registration system that will replace the paper-based system. First, she believes that it'll be easier to make changes to her schedule with the computer-based system. For the university's current system, a professor has to fill out a form whenever a student adds or drops a class. But the computer-based system will allow students to adjust their schedules online, saving them time. Additionally, the woman believes that the new class-confirmation system will be much more convenient than the current, paper confirmations. She claims that she always loses the paper confirmations, and confirmations by email will be easier to keep track of. Moreover, she mentions that sending class confirmations by email will save a lot of paper, benefitting the environment.

Now practice saying your response aloud. If possible, have a friend or a classmate fill out this checklist as you say your response to him or her. If you are by yourself, record and listen to your response, and then fill out the checklist below on your own.

Deliver your response within 60 seconds.

Task 3 Response Checklist

	Yes	Somewhat	No
• Does the speaker summarize the university's proposal?			
• Does the speaker state the student's opinion regarding the university's proposal?			
• Does the speaker list the student's two reasons for agreeing or disagreeing with the proposal?			
• Does the speaker deliver an organized response by using transition words and proper sentence structures?			
• Does the speaker deliver a coherent response by using appropriate tone and pronunciation?			
• Does the speaker finish within the time limit?			

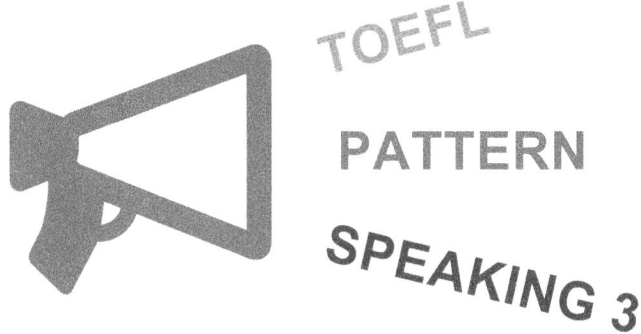

CHAPTER 4

Academic Course
(Reading and Listening)

Chapter 4

Academic Course

GENERAL BACKGROUND INFORMATION

1. EXPLANATION OF TASK 4

Speaking Task 4 requires that you connect the information in an academic passage to the information in a related lecture. You are scored on your ability to clearly integrate and relay important points from the passage and the lecture.

The passage provides a general definition of a term, process, or idea. The lecture covers the same topic, giving examples or detailed information to illustrate the content from the passage. The prompt asks that you combine and relay the main points from the passage and lecture.

For this task, you are given 40 to 50 seconds to read and take notes on the 75- to 100-word passage. The corresponding lecture is 60 to 90 seconds long (150 to 220 words).

After listening to the lecture, read and listen to the prompt, which stays on the screen.

> **Prompt**
> Explain how the examples discussed in the lecture illustrate the main topic presented in the passage.

You are then given 30 seconds of "Preparation Time" to prepare your response and 60 seconds of "Response Time" in which to respond.

The topics discussed in the passage and lecture are taken from a range of areas, such as psychology, history, literature, and biology. The task does not require previous knowledge of any subject.

Although you do not need to include all the information from the passage and lecture, you must provide enough information so that a listener unfamiliar with the passage and lecture would understand your response.

2. NECESSARY SKILLS FOR TASK 4

You must be able to:

- paraphrase subject matter from written and spoken sources
- identify and summarize major point from written and spoken sources
- convey relationships between abstract concepts and concrete information
- connect a spoken example to a written term, process, or concept

HACKING STRATEGY

STEP 1. OUTLINE YOUR RESPONSE

- Take notes as you read the passage
- Take notes as you listen to the lecture
- Read the prompt carefully

STEP 2. PREPARE YOUR RESPONSE

- Summarize the passage and lecture information
- Make sure that you can fully address the prompt

STEP 3. DELIVER YOUR RESPONSE

- Respond with coherent sentences
- Add transition words between ideas

HACKING STRATEGY EXAMPLE

STEP 1. OUTLINE YOUR RESPONSE

Take notes on important information as you read the passage and listen to the corresponding lecture. Do not take notes using full sentences, as you have limited time to complete this step when taking the TOEFL Speaking test.

PASSAGE

Optimism Bias

In psychology, *optimism bias* describes the tendency for people to be overly hopeful about the results of planned actions. Optimism bias includes two parts: one part involves overestimating the chance of positive results, so you think positive events have a bigger chance of occurring than they actually do. Another part involves underestimating the chance of negative results, so you think negative results have a lower chance of occurring than they do. All people are susceptible to optimism bias. Those who achieve the most and have the best attitudes seem to make this misjudgment more frequently.

PASSAGE NOTES

optimism bias: overly hopeful of planned actions

LECTURE

Let me give you two examples of optimism bias.

The first has to do with marriage in the United States. Currently, over half of all marriages in the U.S. end in divorce. Despite this truth, study after study shows that almost all newlyweds say that they'll never get divorced. In effect, their overly positive attitudes about their new marriage—their "optimism bias"—prevents them from seeing any problems down the road.

Another example of the potential dangers of optimism bias is credit card borrowing. Optimism bias causes many people to believe that they'll have more money in the future than they do now, so they spend more money using their credit cards than they can ever pay back. Usually, this doesn't happen during single purchase but over a long period. During a period of several years, people borrow more and more money. Eventually, they have a debt crisis and are forced to confront the reality of their optimism bias.

NOTES

ex. 1: marriage in U.S.
- *more than ½ divorce*
- *newlyweds say never divorce*
- *OB → believe no problem*

ex. 2: credit card
- *borrow more than pay, long time*
- *→ debt crisis, face reality*

Once you have taken notes on the passage and the lecture, carefully read the prompt.

> **Prompt**
>
> Explain optimism bias, focusing on how the examples used by the professor illustrate this concept.

STEP 2. PREPARE YOUR RESPONSE

During the 30-second preparation time, make sure that your notes address all the points in the prompt, and use the information in your notes to organize your response. Because you only have 30 seconds to prepare your response, do not write using complete sentences.

1) Make sure that you can summarize the main idea of the passage.
   From Notes → Main Idea: *optimism bias = overly hopeful of planned actions*

2) Make sure that you can explain the main topic of the lecture.
   From Notes → Topic: *optimism bias*
   　　　　　　　　　Example 1: *marriage in U.S.*
   　　　　　　　　　Example 2: *credit card*

3) Make sure that you can explain how the lecture information relates to the passage.
   From Notes → Details: *(P) optimism bias*
   　　　　　　　　　　(L) marriage: newly weds say never divorce → more than ½ divorce
   　　　　　　　　　　credit card: borrow more than pay → debt

STEP 3. DELIVER YOUR RESPONSE

Use your notes for guidance as you deliver your response. You must deliver your response using complete and coherent sentences. Add transitions to show how ideas relate to one another.

The passage discusses optimism bias, which describes the tendency to be overly hopeful about the results of planned actions. **The professor uses** *marriage and credit card borrowing as examples of this concept.* **First, the professor uses** *divorce rates* **as an example**. *Research shows that over half of married couples in America eventually get divorced. But the majority of newlyweds claim that they'll never get divorced. Because they're so positive, or optimistic, about the outcome of their marriage, the couple firmly believes that they'll never get divorced.* **Next, the professor uses** *credit card borrowing* **as an example**. *Because of their optimism bias, people put more and more money on their credit cards, believing that one day they'll have enough money to pay off their credit card debt. This borrowing occurs little by little, over a long period of time. In the end, those who borrow money have to accept huge debts as the consequences of their actions.*

Task 4

Practice 1

Question 4 of 6

🕒 Reading Time 00:00:45

Attribution Bias

In psychology, an *attribution bias* describes the tendency to unconsciously judge others' actions differently than one judges his or her own actions. Two of the most common types of attribution biases are fundamental attribution errors and actor-observer biases. The *fundamental attribution error* describes the process by which an individual blames another's apparent mistakes on that person's character without considering possible external issues that caused the mistake. Conversely, the *actor-observer bias* occurs because an individual often places blame for his or her apparent errors on external factors rather than on his or her own personality.

Passage Notes

Main Idea: _____

_____

Now listen to part of a lecture on this topic in a psychology class.

Question 4 of 6

Task 4
Your Turn

Lecture Notes

Example 1: _____

_____

Example 2: _____

_____

Question 4 of 6

Explain how the two examples discussed by the professor illustrate differences in the ways people explain behavior.

Preparation Time 00:00:30
Response Time 00:01:00

Response

Task 4

Practice 1

Question 4 of 6

Reading Time 00:00:45

Attribution Bias

In psychology, an *attribution bias* describes the tendency to unconsciously judge others' actions differently than one judges his or her own actions. Two of the most common types of attribution biases are fundamental attribution errors and actor-observer biases. The *fundamental attribution error* describes the process by which an individual blames another's apparent mistakes on that person's character without considering possible external issues that caused the mistake. Conversely, the *actor-observer bias* occurs because an individual often places blame for his or her apparent errors on external factors rather than on his or her own personality.

Passage Notes

Main Idea: *attribution bias*

- others = personal
- self = env.

Now listen to part of a lecture on this topic in a psychology class.

I want to give two examples of attribution bias so that you can better understand this concept. The first example describes an instance of the fundamental attribution error while the second example illustrates the actor-observer bias.

To start, imagine that you're driving to school. While you're carefully getting onto the highway, another driver swerves in your direction from the other side of the highway, almost hitting you. In this situation, what would you think and do? If you were like most people, you'd honk your horn and yell at the driver, and maybe even make a rude hand gesture. You'd probably think to yourself, "What a terrible and careless driver that person is," attributing the action to his personal control instead of an environmental factor.

Now, pretend that you're driving home from school the same evening. You're now on the other side of the freeway. When you get close to your exit, you notice a large hole in the middle of the highway, and you swerve to avoid it. In doing so, you move toward the other side of the highway, barely missing the driver on the other side. This driver honks at you, as you did in the morning. However, if you're like most people, you don't attribute your own swerving to bad driving, but to the hole in the road. This is an environmental factor. Taken together, these examples perfectly represent the two sides of attribution bias.

Task 4
Model Answer

Lecture Notes

Example 1: _drive to school_

• s/b swerve in your side → careless driver (personal)

Example 2: _drive home from school_

• I notice hole & swerve → blame hole (env.)

Question 4 of 6

Explain how the two examples discussed by the professor illustrate differences in the ways people explain behavior.

 Response

According to attribution bias theories, we often consider others' mistakes to be caused by personal failures. But when describing our own actions, we explain them as a product of the environment. The lecture gives two examples to illustrate the theory. First, the professor gives an example of the fundamental-attribution error. He asks the students to imagine that they're driving to school. While driving, another driver from the other side of the highway swerves, almost causing an accident. Professor explains that in this case, most people would attribute the driver's action to personal carelessness without considering any environmental factors that may have led to the incident. Next, the professor asks students to pretend that they're driving home from school. They then notice a hole on the highway, and swerve into the other side of the road, almost hitting an oncoming driver. Professor explains that in this case, most people would attribute their own actions to environmental factors. This example highlights the principles of the actor-observer bias.

Task 4
Practice 2

Question 4 of 6

🕐 Reading Time 00:00:45

Cognitive Dissonance

Cognitive dissonance is one of the most studied phenomena in social psychology. It describes the distress that people feel while holding two conflicting beliefs or ideas simultaneously. In other words, it happens when people perceive a lack of logical consistency between two ideas. When this inconsistency cannot be successfully resolved, people will reduce dissonance by changing one of their ideas. However, people usually do not want to discard either of their conflicting ideas. Hence, many people just make rationalizations and new reasons that support their beliefs.

Passage Notes

Main Idea: _____

_____

Now listen to part of a lecture in a psychology class.

Question 4 of 6

Task 4
Your Turn

Lecture Notes

Example 1: _____

_____

Example 2: _____

_____

Question 4 of 6

Explain how Aesop's fable and the study about doomsday cults illustrate the principle of cognitive dissonance.

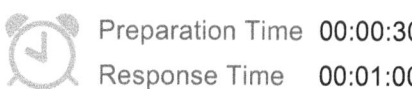

Preparation Time 00:00:30
Response Time 00:01:00

Response

Task 4

Practice 2

Question 4 of 6

Reading Time 00:00:45

Cognitive Dissonance

Cognitive dissonance is one of the most studied phenomena in social psychology. It describes the distress that people feel while holding two conflicting beliefs or ideas simultaneously. In other words, it happens when people perceive a lack of logical consistency between two ideas. When this inconsistency cannot be successfully resolved, people will reduce dissonance by changing one of their ideas. However, people usually do not want to discard either of their conflicting ideas. Hence, many people just make rationalizations and new reasons that support their beliefs.

Passage Notes

Main Idea: _cog. diss._

- 2 opposing ideas → try to resolve

Now listen to part of a lecture in a psychology class.

We've all experienced cognitive dissonance in our lives. When we experience this dissonance, we're likely to do one of two things: change one of our ideas or make new rationalizations for holding two illogical ideas. Let me illustrate cognitive dissonance with a couple of famous examples.

One example comes from the old fable by Aesop called "The Fox and the Grapes." The fable describes a fox that sees some grapes hanging just out of his reach, and he wishes to eat them. However, after several minutes, he can't think of a way to get to these grapes. As a result, he decides that the grapes are not worth eating because they're probably too ripe or too sour. This is an example of resolving cognitive dissonance by creating new rationalizations to justify two conflicting ideas—wanting the grapes but not being able to get them.

Another famous example comes from a 1956 American psychological study of doomsday cults, which are religious cults whose members believe that the world is about to end. The study found that most members of the cults did not abandon their groups even when their expectations for the end of the world weren't met. Instead, cult-members invented new reasons for the world's failure to end, such as claiming that their leader was not a true prophet, or that the leader got the "end of the world" date wrong.

Task 4

Model Answer

Lecture Notes

Example 1: _Aesop's "Fox & Grapes"_

- _fox wants grapes → can't reach → decides grapes taste bad_

Example 2: _doomsday cults (end of world)_

- _no end of world → cults say leader false / date wrong_

Question 4 of 6

Explain how Aesop's fable and the study about doomsday cults illustrate the principle of cognitive dissonance.

 Response

Cognitive dissonance describes a feeling people get when they hold two conflicting ideas. Most people try to rationalize their ideas to resolve this feeling. The lecture gives two examples to illustrate the concept. First, the professor discusses one of Aesop's fables to illustrate cognitive dissonance. When a fox sees grapes hanging out of reach, he wants to eat them. However, he can't reach the grapes, so he decides that they probably taste bad. In the fable, the fox resolves his cognitive dissonance by deciding that his desire is really not that desirable after all. Second, the professor talks about religious cults that believed that the world's end was imminent. When the end of the world didn't come, many members of such cults did not abandon their beliefs. Instead, they simply decided that their leader wasn't the right person, or that the date was wrong.

Task 4

Practice 3

Question 4 of 6

⏱ Reading Time 00:00:45

Mnemonic Devices

Mnemonic devices are techniques that help people memorize information. The method generally involves associating an item that you want to memorize with a word or phrase. When the human mind associates something new with something familiar and meaningful, the new "thing" becomes easier to memorize. The familiar word or phrase must hold personal meaning for the person who uses it to recall information. Interestingly, mnemonic devices often appear random and illogical to outsiders. The key to creating useful mnemonic devices is that the association must make sense to the person using it.

Passage Notes

Main Idea: _____

_____

Now listen to part of a lecture on this topic in a psychology class.

Question 4 of 6

Task 4
Your Turn

Lecture Notes

Example 1: _____

_____

Example 2: _____

_____

Question 4 of 6

Both the passage and lecture discuss mnemonic devices. Using information from the passage and the lecture, describe mnemonic devices and explain some of the ways that they are used.

Preparation Time 00:00:30
Response Time   00:01:00

Response

_____
_____
_____
_____
_____
_____
_____
_____
_____
_____
_____

Practice 3

Question 4 of 6

 Reading Time 00:00:45

Mnemonic Devices

Mnemonic devices are techniques that help people memorize information. The method generally involves associating an item that you want to memorize with a word or phrase. When the human mind associates something new with something familiar and meaningful, the new "thing" becomes easier to memorize. The familiar word or phrase must hold personal meaning for the person who uses it to recall information. Interestingly, mnemonic devices often appear random and illogical to outsiders. The key to creating useful mnemonic devices is that the association must make sense to the person using it.

Passage Notes

Main Idea: _mnemonic devices_

· _memorize things, special word_

Now listen to part of a lecture on this topic in a psychology class.

Let me give you two examples of mnemonic devices. One is commonly used to teach children in elementary school. The other mnemonic device was one that I used to memorize an access code.

Let's start with a mnemonic device that many of you may have learned as children. It's the phrase "Super Man Helps Every One." Here, the first letter of each word corresponds with the order of the Great Lakes from west to east; they are Superior, Michigan, Huron, Erie, and Ontario. Although the phrase "Super Man Helps Every One" has nothing to do with the Great Lakes or geography per se, many children find that this simple phrase helps them memorize the names and the positions of the Great Lakes.

My own mnemonic device relates to an access code that I had to memorize to get into my old laboratory in college. When I got the code—KALNBACBS—it just seemed like a bunch of random letters. However, I realized that by chunking, or dividing the nine letters into three groups of three, I could easily memorize the code. My three groups were KAL, NBA, and CBS. Do you recognize those letters? They are acronyms for a Korean airline, an American professional basketball league, and an American television network. After I chunked my code in this way, I never forgot it.

Task 4
Model Answer

Lecture Notes

Example 1: _Super Man Helps Every One_

• ele. school → Great lakes, west ~ east; help memorize

Example 2: _access code_

• random letters divide 9 → 3 groups (KAL, NBA, CBS) → familiar

---

Question 4 of 6

Both the passage and lecture discuss mnemonic devices. Using information from the passage and the lecture, describe mnemonic devices and explain some of the ways that they are used.

 Response

Mnemonic devices are formed by associating something familiar with something unfamiliar in a memorable way. The professor gives two examples of mnemonic devices in the lecture. First, the professor describes a phrase taught to elementary school children: Super Man Helps Every One. Although this phrase has nothing to do with lakes, it provides a simple way for children to memorize the names and the locations of the five Great Lakes. Next, the professor describes the mnemonic device that he used to memorize an access code. The code was a random nine-letter sequence. However, when he divided it into KAL, NBA, and CBS, he was able to easily remember the code by using familiar associations.

Task 4

Practice 4

Question 4 of 6

⏱ Reading Time 00:00:45

Understanding Sharks

Although they have developed a fearsome reputation, sharks are only responsible for about five human deaths annually. Yet humans are responsible for the deaths of millions of sharks each year, putting many shark species in danger of extinction. There are nearly 500 known shark species, and very few of them fit the popular image of the massive predator that attacks anything it encounters. Ultimately, most shark species are harmless, and they have been wrongly demonized because of their strange, intimidating appearance.

Passage Notes

Main Idea: _____

_____

Now listen to part of a lecture in a biology class.

Question 4 of 6

Task 4
Your Turn

Lecture Notes

Example 1: _____

_____

Example 2: _____

_____

Question 4 of 6

Using information from the passage and examples from the lecture, explain why sharks are misunderstood creatures.

Preparation Time 00:00:30
Response Time   00:01:00

Response

Task 4

Practice 4

Question 4 of 6

Reading Time 00:00:45

Understanding Sharks

Although they have developed a fearsome reputation, sharks are only responsible for about five human deaths annually. Yet humans are responsible for the deaths of millions of sharks each year, putting many shark species in danger of extinction. There are nearly 500 known shark species, and very few of them fit the popular image of the massive predator that attacks anything it encounters. Ultimately, most shark species are harmless, and they have been wrongly demonized because of their strange, intimidating appearance.

Passage Notes

Main Idea: _sharks_

• _over hunted, misunderstood_   • _mostly harmless_

Now listen to part of a lecture in a biology class.

As the reading mentioned, most shark species aren't a threat to humans, and I'll give two examples of shark species that will hopefully get rid of misconceptions about the dangers posed by sharks.

Greenland sharks mostly inhabit the northern seas around Greenland and Iceland. However, specimens have been found as far south as the Gulf of Mexico. These sharks are predators that can grow to be 6.4 meters long, nearly as long as a great white shark. Despite their massive size, they've never been known to attack humans, as they usually prey on large fish or carrion. Preferring cold waters, these sharks usually inhabit depths exceeding 1,000 meters, although they're often found near the ocean's surface during the winter. Because of their freezing environment, Greenland sharks have an incredibly slow metabolism, making them one of the slowest sharks, but also the longest-lived; some researchers estimate that these sharks can live for over 200 years.

Now, let's take a look at goblin sharks. Although the goblin shark looks like an alien, with its long, pointed nose and extendable mouth, it's actually an ancient species distributed throughout the world's oceans. Despite its wide distribution, the goblin shark is poorly understood, as it inhabits depths greater than 100 meters and is rarely captured, making it incredibly difficult to observe or study. However, researchers know that the creature's long nose detects electrical signals that are emitted by its prey, and its mouth can quickly extend outward to capture unsuspecting prey. Despite its 4-meter length and terrifying appearance, this species has never attacked a human.

Lecture Notes

Example 1: _Greenland shark_

• _huge but harmless_ • _deep-sea, cold env._

Example 2: _Goblin shark_

• _look scary but harmless_ • _live in deep, little known_ • _special hunting adaptation_

Question 4 of 6

Using information from the passage and examples from the lecture, explain why sharks are misunderstood creatures.

 Response

The passage discusses the idea that people harm sharks much more than they harm people. And the passage states that sharks' bad reputations are mistaken. The lecture talks about two species of shark that appear terrifying, but don't bother humans. First, the lecture describes Greenland sharks, which are almost as big as great white sharks. Greenland sharks never attack humans, as they live in cold, deep-sea and arctic environments. The professor also points out that these amazing creatures may live for hundreds of years. The lecture also talks about goblin sharks, which look terrifying, but have also never been known to harm humans. These mysterious sharks live deep in the ocean, and they use their strangely shaped noses to seek prey.

Task 4

Practice 5

Question 4 of 6

🕒 Reading Time 00:00:45

The Scientific Method

In the last four centuries, humans have gone from thinking that Earth sits at the center of the universe to understanding that the Earth is simply one of billions of planets sitting at the edge of one of billions of galaxies. This huge leap in understanding our universe is due largely to the development of the scientific method. Essentially, the scientific method is the processes of forming a question based upon observation, forming a possible explanation to the question, testing the explanation for accuracy, and using these test results to confirm or reject your explanation.

Passage Notes

Main Idea: _____
_____

Now listen to part of a lecture on this topic in a physics class.

Question 4 of 6

Task 4
Your Turn

Lecture Notes

Example 1: _____
_____

Example 2: _____
_____

Question 4 of 6

Using information from the passage and the lecture, describe the scientific method and explain how past scientists contributed to its development.

Preparation Time 00:00:30
Response Time 00:01:00

Response

_____
_____
_____
_____
_____
_____
_____
_____
_____
_____

Practice 5

Question 4 of 6

⏱ Reading Time 00:00:45

The Scientific Method

In the last four centuries, humans have gone from thinking that Earth sits at the center of the universe to understanding that the Earth is simply one of billions of planets sitting at the edge of one of billions of galaxies. This huge leap in understanding our universe is due largely to the development of the scientific method. Essentially, the scientific method is the processes of forming a question based upon observation, forming a possible explanation to the question, testing the explanation for accuracy, and using these test results to confirm or reject your explanation.

Passage Notes

Main Idea: _scientific method_

- _advanced sci._   - _theory, testing for accuracy_

Now listen to part of a lecture on this topic in a physics class.

Now that you understand the basic principles of the scientific method, I'd like to present two figures who helped shape the scientific method into the powerful tool it is today.

Before the 17th century, scientific theories were established using logic and thought experiments, or hypothetical situations that explained natural phenomena. However, Italian astronomer and mathematician Galileo Galilei drastically changed the landscape of scientific research. He used mathematics and experimentation to disprove scientific theories that had been accepted for centuries. For example, Galileo's experiments allowed him to accurately predict the rate at which an object in free fall will accelerate, and his findings disproved theories of acceleration that had been around since Aristotle's time. This idea—that controlled experiments can accurately predict natural phenomena—was revolutionary in the 1600s.

Another 17th-century thinker who made great contributions to the development of the scientific method is the English scientist Sir Isaac Newton, who wrote extensively about the proper way to conduct scientific research. While Galileo used experimentation to prove scientific principles, Newton was the first to systematize experimental procedures. His rigid scientific method, which emphasized discovering the causes of phenomena through observation and experimentation, led him to discover the law of universal gravitation, as well as many other scientific principles that forever changed our understanding of the universe.

Task 4
Model Answer

Lecture Notes

Example 1: _Galileo Galilei_

- _used math, exp._
- _discoveries = accurate → disproved old ideas_

Example 2: _Isaac Newton_

- _exp., observe_
- _interested in causes → gravity_

Question 4 of 6

Using information from the passage and the lecture, describe the scientific method and explain how past scientists contributed to its development.

Response

The passage discusses the scientific method, which has greatly advanced our understanding of how the universe works. The passage says that the scientific method is a process of coming up with theories about how things work and testing these theories to see if they're accurate. The lecture talks about scientists who help develop the scientific method. The first scientist mentioned in the lecture is Italian Galileo Galilei, who used math and experiments to show how falling objects accelerate. By doing so, he disproved old theories that used different, less accurate methods to form conclusions. The other figure discussed in the lecture is 17th-century English scientist Isaac Newton, who built upon Galileo's use of experimentation. He wrote a lot about how to find out what causes certain things to happen in nature. Using his scientific method, he discovered how gravity influences objects.

Now practice saying your response aloud. If possible, have a friend/classmate fill out this checklist as you say your response to him or her. If you are by yourself, record and listen to your response, and then fill out the checklist below on your own.

Deliver your response within 60 seconds.

Task 4 Response Checklist

	Yes	Somewhat	No
• Does the speaker accurately summarize the concept discussed in the passage?			
• Does the speaker accurately summarize the example(s) presented in the lecture?			
• Does the speaker explain how the example(s) in the lecture relate to the concept described in the passage?			
• Does the speaker deliver an organized response by using transition words and proper sentence structures?			
• Does the speaker deliver a coherent response by using appropriate tone and pronunciation?			
• Does the speaker finish within the time limit?			

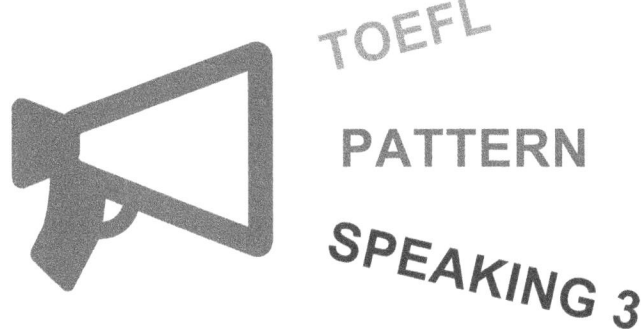

CHAPTER 5

Campus Situation
(Listening)

Chapter 5 Campus Situation

GENERAL BACKGROUND INFORMATION

1. EXPLANATION OF TASK 5

Task 5 requires you to listen to a short conversation that one might hear in a university setting. The conversation will be between a student and another student, a professor, or a university employee.

Some common conversation topics include:

- academic problems (e.g. bad grades, difficulty deciding on a major)
- scheduling conflicts or absences
- financial difficulties

In the conversation, a student will describe a problem that he or she is having, and the other speaker will provide two possible solutions.

After listening to the conversation, you will be given a prompt related to what you have heard. The prompt appears on your computer screen and is read aloud by a narrator.

> **Prompt**
> The speakers discuss two solutions to the man's/woman's problem. Explain what the man's/woman's problem is. Then state which solution you prefer and explain your preference.

When providing a preferred solution in your response, you can either use one of the solutions from the conversation or come up with your own solution. Similarly, when producing reasons to support your preferred solution, you can either use the reasons stated in the conversation or create your own.

After reading the prompt, you have 20 seconds of "Preparation Time" to prepare your response. At the end, you will hear a short beep. The clock then changes to "Response Time" and begins to count down.

You have 60 seconds in which to respond. At the end of the 60 seconds, the recording ends and a new message alerts you that the response time is over.

You may take notes while listening to the conversation and during your preparation time. You also may check your notes when responding to the question.

2. NECESSARY SKILLS FOR TASK 5

You must be able to:

- understand information from spoken sources regarding campus-based subject matter
- identify and summarize major points and important details from spoken sources
- discuss the connection between issues and their proposed solutions

HACKING STRATEGY

STEP 1. Outline Your Response

- Take notes as you listen to the conversation
- Read the prompt carefully

STEP 2. Prepare Your Response

- Explain the student's problem
- State which solution you prefer and why you prefer it

STEP 3. Deliver Your Response

- Respond with coherent sentences
- Add transition words between ideas

HACKING STRATEGY EXAMPLE

STEP 1. OUTLINE YOUR RESPONSE

Take notes on important information as you listen to the conversation. Do not take notes using full sentences, as you will not have time to do so.

CONVERSATION

A: Hello, University Housing Office. How may I help you?

FS: Hi, I have a question about spring break. I was wondering if students can stay in their dorm rooms during the break.

A: Oh, I see, well, are you living in a residence hall or a student apartment right now?

FS: A residence hall.

A: OK, residence halls are closed during spring break, as are all the dining facilities. I'm afraid you'll have to go home for vacation.

FS: The problem is that spring break is only a week, and I live so far away that flying home would be too expensive. And all of my friends are going home.

A: Well, unfortunately, you'll have to find somewhere else to stay. I can give you a couple of suggestions. One is that you could go to the Student Center and check the bulletin boards. I noticed that some students or instructors who live off-campus are advertising for house-sitters for spring break.

FS: Umm, well, I'm not sure. What do house-sitters do?

A: Well, they live in the house and take care of the plants and the pets while the owner is away. You could use the kitchen, so you'd save money. They might even pay you. It'd be a way of having a nice, quiet spring break.

FS: I suppose, but it might be too quiet. I don't know what to do.

A: Another idea is that you could go on a road trip. Maybe one of your friends would like to go with you, and you could visit other friends at their family homes.

FS: Yeah, that sounds fun. I'd have to rent a car, though.

A: I think it'd be cheaper than a plane ticket home.

FS: I hope so! Well, thank you for the suggestions.

A: You're welcome.

A: Advisor / **FS:** Female Student

NOTES

P *dorm closed on vacation*
- *too expensive to fly home*
- *friends going home*
- *no place to stay*

S1 *house-sitting → practical*
- *save/earn $*
- *may be bored, lonely*

S2 *road trip*
- *sightseeing*
- *better friendships*
- *afford rental?*
- *worthwhile*

After taking notes, carefully read the prompt, making sure that you know exactly what it asks you to do.

> **Prompt**
>
> Briefly summarize the problem that the speakers discuss. Then state which of the two solutions from the conversation you would recommend. Explain the reasons for your recommendation.

STEP 2. PREPARE YOUR RESPONSE 00:00:20

During the 20-second preparation time, make sure that your notes address all the points in the prompt, and use the information in your notes to organize your response. Because you only have 20 seconds to prepare your response, do not write using complete sentences.

1) Make sure that you can summarize the student's problem.
   From Notes → Problem: *woman no housing for spring break*

2) Make sure that you can identify which of the two proposed solutions you prefer.
   Preferred solution: *take a road trip*

3) Make sure that you can give two reasons explaining why you prefer this solution.
   Reason 1: *taking care of pets → can be boring and lonely*
   Reason 2: *do sight-seeing, get to know friends better*

STEP 3. DELIVER YOUR RESPONSE 00:01:00

Use the outline that you created in STEP 2 to guide you as you deliver your response. Respond using complete sentences, and add transition words to show how ideas relate to one another.

> *The student's problem is that she lives in a residence hall on campus, but it'll be closed during spring break. It would be too expensive to fly home for only one week, and her friends are all going home. **Thus**, she doesn't have a place to stay during the break. **The advisor suggests that** she either respond to some ads for housesitting in the community, or take a road trip to visit friends. **I definitely think she should** take a road trip. If she's able to find a house-sitting job, she'll save money because she'll have a place to stay for free. She may even get paid. But, taking care of the pets will mean staying there the whole week, and she might get very bored and lonely. **I think** that planning a road trip to visit friends from school would be ideal. She'd get to do some sight-seeing and get to know her friends better by staying in their family homes. If she can afford to rent a car, I think she'd have a worthwhile experience.*

Task 5
Practice 1

Listen to part of a conversation between two students.

Question 5 of 6

Conversation Notes

Problem: _____

Solution 1: _____

Solution 2: _____

Task 5
Your Turn

Preparation Notes

Preference: _____

Reasons: _____

_____

_____

Question 5 of 6

The students discuss two possible solutions to the man's problem. Describe the problem. Then state which solution you prefer and explain why you prefer it.

Preparation Time 00:00:20
Response Time 00:01:00

🔊 **Response**

_____
_____
_____
_____
_____
_____
_____
_____
_____
_____

Task 5
Practice 1

Listen to part of a conversation between two students.

F: Are your parents still giving you a hard time about your major?

M: Yeah, my dad wants me to study engineering, but I'm not backing down. I want to be a musician.

F: Good for you. You've got to pursue your passion.

M: But I'm having trouble with the stress. My dad is threatening to cut off my funds for college, and, well, I don't really know what to do anymore.

F: Oh, gosh. You know, maybe you should talk to someone. They have great psychologists at the university counseling center.

M: Yeah? I guess they could provide me with some support.

F: Oh, definitely. I went there after my boyfriend broke up with me, and they really helped me a lot.

M: Hmm, yeah, I think I could use some moral support. But, I don't think a couple of psychologists can solve the problem itself. I mean, what else would they do except just listen to me? After all, it's a problem between me and my father.

F: Well, then maybe you should stop accepting money from your parents. You could take out a student loan or apply for some grants.

M: Hmm, I don't know about that. Wouldn't it be too hard on me? I've never done anything like that in my whole life.

F: I know. Well, think about it.

F: Female Student / M: Male Student

Conversation Notes

Problem: *deciding major: dad → engineering / man → musician (dad say no more $)*

Solution 1: *talk to psych.*

Solution 2: *stop taking money from dad*

Task 5
Model Answer

Preparation Notes

Preference: _talk to psych._

Reasons: • _find good solution_

• _stop taking money: dad → angrier_

Question 5 of 6

The students discuss two possible solutions to the man's problem. Describe the problem. Then state which solution you prefer and explain why you prefer it.

 **Response**

The man's problem is that he wants to be a musician, but his father wants him to major in engineering. His father has even threatened to stop his financial contributions. The woman comes up with two solutions: talk to a psychologist or stop taking money from his parents. I think the man should talk to a psychologist before doing anything else. First, the woman guarantees that the school psychologists are helpful. She herself benefited from their services. Although the man believes it wouldn't help him solve the problem, I'm sure that he'd find an acceptable solution after discussing his issues with a professional. Therefore, I believe that talking to a counselor is the best option. Plus, not accepting money would be too hard on the man. And doing so might make his father even angrier, thus making the bad situation far worse.

Task 5
Practice 2

Listen to part of a conversation between two students.

Question 5 of 6

Conversation Notes

Problem: _____

Solution 1: _____

Solution 2: _____

Task 5
Your Turn

Preparation Notes

Preference: _____

Reasons: _____

_____

_____

Question 5 of 6

The students discuss two possible solutions to the woman's problem. Describe the problem. Then state which solution you prefer and explain why you prefer it.

Preparation Time   00:00:20
Response Time   00:01:00

Response

Practice 2

Listen to part of a conversation between two students.

F: Hey, Mike. I'm having a problem with one of my professors and I don't know what to do about it.

M: Yeah? What's going on?

F: Well, it's his tests. Almost everyone from the class thinks that they're unfair. For example, he'll lecture on one topic for a couple of weeks. But when he gives us a test, it doesn't really cover the material he has lectured on.

M: Oh, that really does sound unfair. Have you tried talking to him about the situation?

F: No. Some other students from my class did that, and the professor just made the next test even more difficult.

M: Wow, that's crazy. Who is this guy, anyway?

F: His name is Professor Johnson. He teaches lower-division chemistry classes.

M: Oh, my gosh! Professor Johnson? Is that guy still here? I had him for a chemistry class as a freshman and he was horrible. In fact, many of the students in my class complained to the administration in an effort to get him fired.

F: Wow, really? I can't believe he wasn't fired back then!

M: You know what? You might want to try complaining to the administration again with other students. Perhaps they'll finally decide to take some action with this lousy professor.

F: Yeah, maybe you're right. Or maybe my actions will just make the professor angrier, and he'll end up making the tests way more difficult.

F: Female Student / M: Male Student

Conversation Notes

Problem: _prob. w/ prof. → test not fair, diff. from lecture_

Solution 1: _talk to prof._

Solution 2: _complain to admin._

Task 5
Model Answer

Preparation Notes

Preference: _complain to admin._

Reasons: _• may fire him_

• take the lead, for other stud.

Question 5 of 6

The students discuss two possible solutions to the woman's problem. Describe the problem. Then state which solution you prefer and explain why you prefer it.

 **Response**

The woman's problem is that she has a professor who gives unfair tests. The man advises the woman to either talk to her professor or submit an official complaint to the administration. In my opinion, the woman should submit an official complaint. First, according to the woman, talking to the professor personally will do no good. Other students from the class tried to reason with the professor, but the professor ended up making the tests harder. Second, the administration needs to know that this professor is still performing poorly. I understand that she's afraid to do this, but I believe that she should take the lead and tell the administration. By doing so, other students will no longer suffer from the professor's unprofessional methods.

Task 5

Practice 3

Listen to part of a conversation between two students.

Question 5 of 6

Conversation Notes

Problem: _____

Solution 1: _____

Solution 2: _____

Task 5
Your Turn

Preparation Notes

Preference: _____

Reasons: _____

_____

_____

Question 5 of 6

The students discuss two possible solutions to the man's problem. Describe the problem. Then state which solution you prefer and explain why you prefer it.

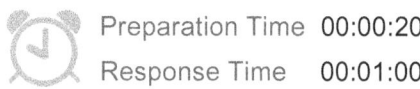

Preparation Time 00:00:20
Response Time   00:01:00

Response

_____
_____
_____
_____
_____
_____
_____
_____
_____
_____
_____

Practice 3

Listen to part of a conversation between two students.

M: Hey, Tess. Have you noticed that the campus computer center closes at 6 pm every day of the week?

F: Yeah, I've noticed that. Why do you ask, Henry?

M: Well, 6 pm seems way too early to me. I mean, when am I supposed to do research and write my papers?

F: Well, maybe you can do your school work in the morning or afternoon, or you could do it during the weekends. After all, the computer center is open seven days a week.

M: You do have a point there. But it's just that, well, I work in the afternoon three days a week, and I like to exercise on the weekends.

F: Oh, I see. Well, have you thought about buying your own computer? I mean, you can get a pretty good one for only a few hundred dollars. You know, computers aren't that expensive these days.

M: Yeah, that's true. But I don't have much money in my budget this year. After paying all of my bills, I'm pretty much broke.

F: Broke, eh? What about all the baseball games you attend? I'm sure the money saved from skipping a few of those could buy you a decent computer.

M: Hmm, I didn't even think about that. I do love baseball, but it's definitely something to consider. Thanks for the suggestions.

M: Male Student / F: Female Student

Conversation Notes

Problem: _comp. center close too early_

Solution 1: _use comp. center (mornings/afternoons/weekends)_

Solution 2: _buy own comp._

Task 5
Model Answer

Preparation Notes

Preference: _buy own comp._

Reasons: * _affordable if ↓ baseball games_

* _computer: must-have item, more important_

Question 5 of 6

The students discuss two possible solutions to the man's problem. Describe the problem. Then state which solution you prefer and explain why you prefer it.

 Response

The man's problem is that the computer center is not open at night. He feels that the evening is the only time he can do his schoolwork. The woman gives the man two options: adjust his schedule so he can use the computer center during its normal hours, or buy his own computer. In my opinion, the man should definitely buy his own computer. First, buying a computer will allow him to finish his schoolwork at his convenience, which is important because of his work and exercise schedule. Second, he can afford to buy a computer. As the woman mentioned, he can save money by not attending baseball games. Personally, I think a computer is a must-have item these days for all students, and owning one is way more important than enjoying some baseball games. I even think that he should work at his job more often so that he can save up and buy a computer of his own.

Task 5
Practice 4

Listen to part of a conversation between two students.

Question 5 of 6

Conversation Notes

Problem: _____

Solution 1: _____

Solution 2: _____

Task 5
Your Turn

Preparation Notes

Preference: _____

Reasons: _____

_____

_____

Question 5 of 6

The students discuss two possible solutions to the man's problem. Describe the problem. Then state which solution you prefer and explain why you prefer it.

 Preparation Time   00:00:20
Response Time   00:01:00

Response

_____
_____
_____
_____
_____
_____
_____
_____
_____
_____

Practice 4

Listen to a part of a conversation between two students.

F: Hey, Mitch. I didn't see you in class this week. Is everything okay?

M: Oh hey, Betty. Yeah, uh, I guess everything is okay. I've just been feeling really homesick lately.

F: Uh-oh, I know how that goes. It sounds like you've got a case of the "freshman blues."

M: Well, maybe so. I've definitely had a hard time getting myself out of bed the last few days. And I've called my parents at least 10 times this week.

F: Wow, you really are homesick! Hey, I don't mean to give unwanted advice, but have you considered talking to one of the on-campus counselors?

M: No, not really. Do you think it might be worthwhile for me to do that?

F: Oh, definitely. Those university counselors helped me get through my homesickness when I was a freshman two years ago. In fact, if it weren't for them, I might've even dropped out of school.

M: Really? I'm glad they were able to help you out so much.

F: Uh-huh. Do you know what else I've noticed about you? You haven't gotten involved in any on-campus activities outside of class. I mean, do you do anything besides go to class, study, and sleep?

M: Well, uh, no, I guess I don't.

F: That's what I thought. I think that's another reason you're feeling homesick. You need to get out more, join a school club, and have some fun.

M: Oh, I don't know about that. I've always been kind of shy.

F: But that's exactly why you need to get out more! It'll help take your mind off your worries and cares.

F: Female Student / M: Male Student

Conversation Notes

Problem: _feeling homesick_

Solution 1: _talk to univ. counselor_

Solution 2: _get out, meet ppl. (school club)_

Task 5

Model Answer

Preparation Notes

Preference: _talk to univ. counselor_

Reasons: * _serious → need professional help_

* _get out, meet ppl. → maybe more depressed, lonely_

Question 5 of 6

The students discuss two possible solutions to the man's problem. Describe the problem. Then state which solution you prefer and explain why you prefer it.

 Response

The man's problem is that he's feeling homesick. The woman suggests that he talk to a counselor or socialize more often. In my opinion, the man should talk to a university counselor. First, talking to a counselor helped the woman when she was suffering from homesickness during her freshman year, so doing so will probably help the man, too. Second, it sounds to me like the man's homesickness is serious and interfering with his ability to go to class. Therefore, I think he needs to get some professional help. Furthermore, the woman suggests that he go out and socialize, but it's not easy for a shy person to meet people. In fact, meeting people could make him even more depressed because he might feel lonelier among people who seem happy.

Task 5

Practice 5

Listen to part of a conversation between two students.

Conversation Notes

Problem: _____

Solution 1: _____

Solution 2: _____

Task 5
Your Turn

Preparation Notes

Preference: _____

Reasons: _____

_____

_____

Question 5 of 6

The students discuss two possible solutions to the woman's problem. Describe the problem. Then state which solution you prefer and explain why you prefer it.

Preparation Time 00:00:20
Response Time 00:01:00

Response

Task 5

Practice 5

Listen to part of a conversation between two students.

M: So, Theresa, have you decided on what major you want to study?

F: No, I haven't, Frank. And I'm really starting to get worried. It's my junior year and I still can't make up my mind.

M: Huh. Are you still taking a lot of art and biology classes?

F: Yeah, I am. Those are the two subjects that I'm really interested in. I've loved both of them since I was a little kid.

M: Why don't you try to double major in both subjects, then? It might take a little longer to graduate, but if that's where your heart is, follow it!

F: Yeah, I guess that's a good way to look at it. Only I'm not sure what kind of job I could get with a double major in biology and art.

M: Well, you're a bright person, so I'm certain that you'll figure something out.

F: I hope so.

M: Oh, do you know what else you might want to look into? Meet with an academic counselor. They're all really knowledgeable about everything major-related.

F: Really? Have you used their services before?

M: Yes, I have. In fact, without their help I never would've been able to choose a major for myself.

F: Wow! That's a persuasive recommendation. Maybe I'll have to check out the academic counseling center for myself.

F: Female Student / **M:** Male Student

Conversation Notes

Problem: _problem: can't decide major_

Solution 1: _• like both art & bio_

Solution 2: _____

Task 5

Model Answer

Preparation Notes

Preference: _do double major_

Reasons: • _follow heart_

• _bio. textbook illustrator_

• _counselor → don't know much, mistake_

Question 5 of 6

The students discuss two possible solutions to the woman's problem. Describe the problem. Then state which solution you prefer and explain why you prefer it.

 Response

The woman's problem is that she can't decide on a major. The man suggests that she double major in biology and art, or that she talk to an academic counselor. In my opinion, the woman should pursue a double major. First, biology and art are the two subjects she's loved all her life, and everyone must pursue his or her passion to be happy in life. Although she worries about her future job prospects, I think she can find a career that uses at least one of the two skills, like becoming a technician at a lab. Or she can even try combining both skills and become a biology textbook illustrator. In addition, counselors don't know the woman as well as she knows herself, so they might mistakenly recommend that she pursue something that she's really not that interested in. If the woman ends up studying a major that she's not passionate about, her whole college experience might be ruined.

Now practice saying your response aloud. If possible, have a friend/classmate fill out this checklist as you say your response to him or her. If you are by yourself, record and listen to your response, and then fill out the checklist below on your own.

Deliver your response within 60 seconds.

Task 5 Response Checklist

	Yes	Somewhat	No
• Does the speaker explain the problem discussed in the conversation?			
• Does the speaker state which of the two proposed solutions he or she prefers?			
• Does the speaker explain why he or she selected this preferred solution?			
• Does the speaker deliver an organized response by using transition words and proper sentence structures?			
• Does the speaker deliver a coherent response by using appropriate tone and pronunciation?			
• Does the speaker finish within the time limit?			

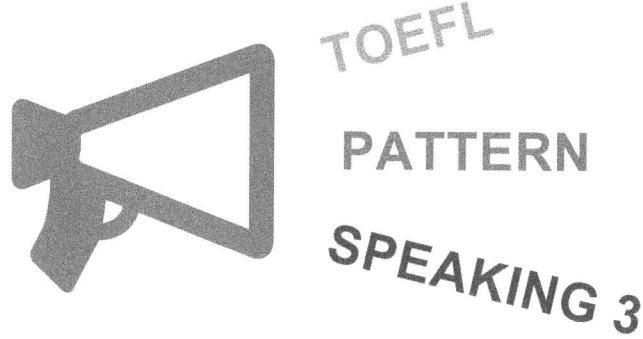

CHAPTER 6

Academic Course
(Listening)

Academic Course

GENERAL BACKGROUND INFORMATION

1. **EXPLANATION OF TASK 6**

   Speaking Task 6 requires you to listen to a brief lecture on an academic subject. The lecture lasts about 90 to 120 seconds and is about 230 to 280 words. The lecture describes a term or concept using academic details or examples. Topics are taken from a range of fields in the life sciences, humanities, social sciences, and physical sciences.

   After you listen to the lecture, instructions will inform you to get ready to respond to the prompt. The prompt will then appear on screen and be read aloud by a narrator.

   The task 6 prompt will ask you to describe the main concept or issue of the lecture and use points or examples from the lecture to support the main idea.

   > **Prompt**
   > Using points and examples from the lecture, explain the topic discussed in the lecture.

   After listening to the prompt, begin preparing your response. A clock below the prompt will count down. You will have 20 seconds to prepare. At the end, you will hear a short beep.

   The clock then changes to "Response Time" and begins to count down. You have 60 seconds to respond. At the end of the 60 seconds, the recording ends and a new message alerts you that the response time is over.

   You will need to use citation language, summarizing, paraphrasing, and transitions for this task.

2. **NECESSARY SKILLS FOR TASK 6**

   You must be able to:
   - identify and summarize major points from a spoken source of information
   - paraphrase information from spoken sources of information
   - relate specific examples to a general topic generated from spoken sources of information

HACKING STRATEGY

STEP 1. OUTLINE YOUR RESPONSE

- Take notes as you listen to the lecture
- Read the prompt carefully

STEP 2. PREPARE YOUR RESPONSE

- Summarize the lecture's main idea
- State how the examples in the lecture relate to the main idea or to each other

STEP 3. DELIVER YOUR RESPONSE

- Respond with coherent sentences
- Add transition words between ideas

HACKING STRATEGY EXAMPLE

STEP 1. OUTLINE YOUR RESPONSE

Take notes on important information as you listen to the lecture. Do not take notes using full sentences, as you will not have time to do so.

> **LECTURE**
>
> Today, I'd like to talk about a marketing strategy almost all companies use. Interestingly, this marketing strategy has nothing to do with television commercials or print advertisements. In fact, it has to do with pricing. Believe it or not, the price that companies set for the product is one of the most important marketing decisions that they can make. There are two different approaches that companies may take when marketing a product through pricing.
>
> A popular approach is to price an item high and then lower its price over time. This marketing strategy is very important with technology. Think of how expensive your computer or cell phone was several years ago, when it first came out. Today, these same products have likely lost one-third to one-half their value. But what makes this a good marketing strategy? Well, customers associate high price with high quality, especially in the world of technology. Thus, if a new computer or cell phone comes out and it's priced too low, people are less likely to buy it because they'll think that it's of low quality.
>
> Another popular approach is the opposite: starting a product with a low price and raising the price over time. This approach is often used with a product that's completely new to the market, such as a new brand of detergent or cleaner. When a new product like this appears at a cheap price, customers are enticed to buy it. Then, over time, as desire for the product becomes higher, the company can raise the price appropriately.

NOTES

T *pricing = marketing tool*
2 approaches

NOTES

D1 *high price → lower (esp. tech. comp, cell)*
- *high $ → good tech.*
- *low $ → bad tech.*

D2 *low → higher*
- *new prod. = detergent*
- *cheap → entice*
- *familiar → raise*

After taking notes, carefully read the prompt, making sure that you know exactly what it asks you to do.

> **Prompt**
> Using points and details from the lecture, describe two different marketing approaches that companies use.

STEP 2. PREPARE YOUR RESPONSE

During the 20-second preparation time, make sure that your notes address all the points in the prompt, and use the information in your notes to organize your response. Because you only have 20 seconds to prepare your response, do not write using complete sentences.

1) Make sure that you can summarize the main idea of the lecture.
    From Notes → Main Idea: *marketing strategy*

2) Make sure that you can explain the first subtopic presented in the lecture.
    From Notes → Subtopic 1: *high price → lower; especially technology (computers, cell phones)*
    high price → good technology; low price → bad technology

3) Make sure that you can explain the second subtopic presented in the lecture.
    From Notes → Subtopic 2: *low price → higher; when product is new (detergent, cleaner)*
    cheap price → ↑ customer demand → ↑ price

STEP 3. DELIVER YOUR RESPONSE

Use the outline that you created in STEP 2 to guide you as you deliver your response. Respond using complete sentences, and add transition words to show how ideas relate to one another.

The professor talks about how the pricing of consumer products can be used as a marketing tool. According to the lecture, there are two approaches: one approach sets a high price for a product that lowers over time, and the other approach sets a low price for a product that increases over time. First, he talks about starting a product at a high price and then lowering it. This approach works well with technology, such as cell phones and computers, because consumers associate high price with high quality in terms of technology. So pricing these products too low scares away customers, as they'll believe they're buying a low-quality item. However, sometimes companies take the opposite approach when pricing products. With a product that's new to the market, such as a new brand of detergent, pricing must be low to entice customers. Then, after customers like the product, the company can raise the price.

Task 6

Practice 1

Now listen to part of a lecture in an ecology class.

Question 6 of 6

Lecture Notes

Main Idea: _____

Subtopic 1: _____

Details: _____

_____

Subtopic 2: _____

Details: _____

_____

Task 6
Your Turn

Question 6 of 6

Using points and examples from the lecture, explain the two causes of species endangerment discussed in the lecture.

Preparation Time 00:00:20
Response Time 00:01:00

Response

Task 6

Practice 1

Now listen to part of a lecture in an ecology class.

Today, I want to talk about some reasons that many animal species have become endangered. As you may know, thousands of animal species are in danger of becoming extinct. Most animal species that go extinct today do so as a result of human activities. Two major factors that cause animal extinction are the loss of natural habitats and competition with domesticated, nonnative animals.

The main threat to the survival of many animals today is the loss of their natural habitats. Forests and marshlands are cleared for agriculture and building projects. Consequently, more and more wild animals lose the majority of their habitats to human invaders. Even worse, once a habitat has been damaged, it rarely returns to its normal state, so animals living in such habitats have virtually no chance of survival.

Another threat to animal survival in native habitats is competition from domesticated, nonnative animals. This problem has especially increased since the 1600s, when world travel became more common. At that time, travelers began introducing animals such as horses, cattle, pigs, and birds into new environments. For example, the introduction of cats into New Zealand in the mid-1800s disrupted the ecosystem, contributing to the extinction of many native bird species.

Lecture Notes

Main Idea: _endangered ani. species / 2 causes for ani. extinction_

Subtopic 1: _loss of habitat_

Details: _• cleared for agri., building_
• wild ani., no place to live (destroy → no return)

Subtopic 2: _nonnative ani._

Details: _• 1600s, world travel → spread cattle, pigs_
• New Zealand cats → extinct. of native birds

Task 6
Model Answer

Question 6 of 6

Using points and examples from the lecture, explain the two causes of species endangerment discussed in the lecture.

Response

In the lecture, the professor says that many animals face extinction because of human activities. The lecture discusses the following two causes—loss of habitat and competition from nonnative animals. First, the professor says that loss of habitat is the main reason many animal species are endangered. Land has been cleared for human developments and agriculture, which reduce or eliminate the habitats of many wild animals. Moreover, once these habitats are destroyed or altered, they rarely return to their natural states. Next, the professor says that domesticated, nonnative animals threaten many animal species. This problem has increased since the 1600s, when world travel became popular. For instance, in the mid-19th century, settlers introduced domesticated cats into New Zealand. These cats' hunting activities led to the extinction of many native bird species.

Task 6
Practice 2

Now listen to part of a lecture in a literature class.

Lecture Notes

Main Idea: _____

Subtopic 1: _____

Details: _____

_____

Subtopic 2: _____

Details: _____

_____

Task 6
Your Turn

Question 6 of 6

The professor talks about pen names. Using examples and details from the lecture, summarize what the professor says about the reasons that authors use pen names.

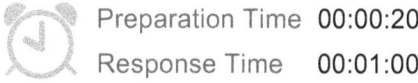

Preparation Time 00:00:20
Response Time 00:01:00

Response

Task 6

Practice 2

Now listen to part of a lecture in a literature class.

Today, I'd like to talk about something that's rarely discussed in literature classes. It's the use of pen names, which are false names adopted by authors. There are many reasons why authors use pen names when publishing their works. Let's focus on a couple of the more popular reasons that authors use pen names in order to better understand this concept.

First, many authors have used pen names to avoid sexual discrimination. We're about to read a novel by the British author George Eliot. As you know, George Eliot wasn't a man, but a woman whose real name was Mary Ann Evans. She wrote under a masculine pen name to avoid the sexual discrimination prevalent in 19th century Victorian England. At this time, few women received the education necessary to become authors, and many people ignored women's opinions and perspectives. Thus, the few women who became authors often used male pen names, and the trend peaked among female authors in Europe and North America during the early- to mid-19th century.

Another historical reason that authors have used pen names was to avoid persecution for writing about controversial subjects. For example, the 18th century French writer Francois-Marie Arouet adopted the pen name Voltaire. This false name allowed him to write critically about religious intolerance—Voltaire was a big critic of the Catholic Church—and other controversial issues in French society at that time without fear of punishment.

Lecture Notes

Main Idea: _pen names 2 reasons_

Subtopic 1: _avoid sex discrimination_

Details: • _George Elliot, woman not man_

• _women not well respected in 19th Euro., N America → use pen names_

Subtopic 2: _write controv. subjects_

Details: • _18th c., Voltaire → criticize religion, other subjects w/o trouble_

Task 6

Model Answer

Question 6 of 6

The professor talks about pen names. Using examples and details from the lecture, summarize what the professor says about the reasons that authors use pen names.

 Response

In the lecture, the professor discusses two reasons that authors use pen names. One reason is to avoid sexual discrimination, and the other is to write freely about controversial issues. To illustrate the use of pen names to avoid sexual discrimination, he mentions British author Mary Ann Evans, who used the masculine pen name George Eliot. During the 19th century in Europe and North America, many female authors felt their works would be ignored if they published their works using a woman's name, as women were not well respected at this time. Thus, these female authors often published works under male names. Next, the professor says that some authors use pen names so that they can write freely about controversial subjects. The 18th century French writer who was known as Voltaire is a prime example of this. By using a pen name, Voltaire was able to criticize religion and other controversial topics in France without getting in trouble.

Task 6
Practice 3

Now listen to part of a lecture in a biology class.

Question 6 of 6

Lecture Notes

Main Idea: _____

Subtopic 1: _____

Details: _____
_____

Subtopic 2: _____

Details: _____
_____

Task 6
Your Turn

Question 6 of 6

Using points and examples from the lecture, describe the two different definitions of life given by the professor.

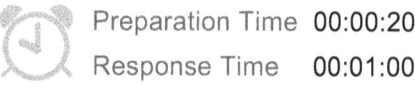

Preparation Time 00:00:20
Response Time 00:01:00

Response

Task 6

Practice 3

Now listen to part of a lecture in a biology class.

Believe it or not, scientists still have trouble agreeing on a clear definition for "life." Of course, all of us probably believe that we can differentiate life from non-life in some way. But when you really start analyzing the qualities of living and non-living things carefully, the problem becomes evident. Let me briefly give two definitions of life—one very ancient, the other very modern.

One ancient theory of life is called the materialist view. Beginning in the 5th century BCE, many Greek philosophers contributed to the materialist view of life, which states that all matter is composed of combinations of four "elements"—earth, fire, water, and air. One of these philosophers, Democritus, wanted to determine what exactly made something "alive." Because the living things he observed were usually warm and able to move, he believed that all living matter contains "fiery atoms," which were basically what we today consider a soul.

Many European intellectuals held this materialist view of matter until the 17th and 18th centuries. During these centuries, Europe underwent a scientific revolution, which gave rise to the "biological" view of life. Unlike the materialist view, the biological view of life doesn't rely on just four "elements," and discards the concept of a soul when considering the qualities of living things. However, exactly what characteristics something must possess to be "alive" is still a matter of scientific debate. But according to the biological view, some well-established characteristics of living things are the abilities to grow and reproduce.

Lecture Notes

Main Idea: _life = diff. to define_

Subtopic 1: _ancient, materialist (Democritus)_

Details: _• 4 ele. (earth, fire, H2O, air)_

• life → "fiery atoms" (ancient) = soul (modern)

Subtopic 2: _modern, biological_

Details: _• ↑ ele., no soul_

• life → grow, reproduce

Task 6

Model Answer

Question 6 of 6

Using points and examples from the lecture, describe the two different definitions of life given by the professor.

 Response

The professor talks about some difficulties of defining "life." According to the lecture, two descriptions of life are the materialist view, which is thousands of years old, and the biological view, which developed fairly recently. First, the professor talks about the ancient Greek materialist definition of life. People who held this view believed that all living things were made up of a combination of water, air, fire, and earth. The philosopher named Democritus claimed that some combinations of matter contained "fiery atoms," and these atoms are what gave things life. Next, the professor talks about the modern biological view of life, which states that all living things share unique characteristics, such as the abilities to grow and reproduce. However, the biological view of life is constantly undergoing change, so some characteristics of life may be added or altered in the future.

Task 6
Practice 4

Now listen to part of a lecture in a biology class.

Lecture Notes

Main Idea: _____

Subtopic 1: _____

Details: _____

_____

Subtopic 2: _____

Details: _____

_____

Task 6
Your Turn

Question 6 of 6

Using points and examples from the lecture, explain the two functions of animal coloration discussed in the lecture.

Preparation Time 00:00:20
Response Time 00:01:00

Response

Task 6

Practice 4

Now listen to part of a lecture in a biology class.

When we look at animals, one of the first things we notice about them is their coloration. In fact, many of us probably form our early opinions about animals due to the way their colors attract or repel us. However, animals' colors serve a far greater purpose than simply giving pleasure or displeasure to humans. In fact, many species' coloration serves one of two purposes—camouflage or warning. Let's talk about both of those right now.

First, there's camouflage, which describes coloration that allows animals to blend into their background. Such colors make animals difficult to be seen in their environments. Interestingly, camouflage can act both as a defensive and aggressive adaptation. For instance, the familiar black and white stripes of African zebras allow them to blend into the grass. This defensive adaptation allows zebras to conceal themselves from lions, which are color-blind. On the other hand, certain spiders blend into their environments so that they can hide from and more easily catch their prey. This is an aggressive type of camouflage.

Second, there's animal coloration as warning, which makes animals stand out from their background as a warning to enemies. In effect, warning coloration makes animals more likely to be remembered in the future. One of the most venomous snakes in North America, the coral snake, has a very noticeable red, orange, and black coloration. This snake, which has no problem obtaining food, is brightly colored to warn other animals. The warning is that if other animals bother or try to prey on the snake, they'll likely die from its venomous bite.

Lecture Notes

Main Idea: _animal coloration_

Subtopic 1: _camouflage, blending_

Details: • _defensive (ex. zebra)_

• _aggressive (ex. spiders)_

Subtopic 2: _warning_

Details: • _stand out, memorable (ex. coral snake)_

Question 6 of 6

Using points and examples from the lecture, explain the two functions of animal coloration discussed in the lecture.

 Response

The professor talks about animal coloration. According to the lecture, animal coloration may serve one of two important purposes—camouflage or warning. One purpose of animal coloration is camouflage. Animals with camouflage coloration blend in with their backgrounds. Some animals possess this coloration as a defensive measure. For example, a zebra's striped coloration disguises it from lions. Other animals develop camouflage for aggressive purposes. For instance, certain spiders use camouflage to sneak up on unsuspecting prey. Another purpose of animal coloration is to warn other animals to stay away from them. Animals with warning coloration try to stand out from their environment, and their coloration makes them memorable to other animals. One example is the black, orange, and red coral snake. The coral snake's bright colors warn other animals to stay away or risk death. This coloration deters potential predators.

Task 6

Practice 5

Now listen to part of a lecture in a linguistics class.

Question 6 of 6

Lecture Notes

Main Idea: _____

Subtopic 1: _____

Details: _____

_____

Subtopic 2: _____

Details: _____

_____

Task 6
Your Turn

Question 6 of 6

Using information from the lecture, describe loaded language and summarize the two uses of loaded language discussed in the lecture.

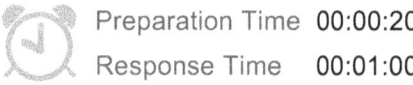
Preparation Time 00:00:20
Response Time 00:01:00

Response

Task 6

Practice 5

Now listen to part of a lecture in a linguistics class.

Let's talk about a linguistic concept known as "loaded language." As the name implies, loaded language describes language that's weighed down, or "loaded," with words that appeal to audiences' emotions. This emotional wording is intentional and meant to influence listeners or readers by manipulating their feelings. Thus, many politicians and advertisers use loaded language that elicits positive feelings to rally public support for a cause or a product; conversely, they'll use language loaded with negative connotations to criticize an opponent or their product. Now let's look more closely at examples of groups that use loaded language to elicit a positive or negative reaction from others.

On the one hand, many wars and conflicts are fueled by appealing to the emotions of the soldiers as well as the public, so all governments involved in a war will use loaded language to dehumanize their enemies. For instance, America's anti-German propaganda often described German soldiers as "monsters" or "brutes." In doing so, the propaganda hoped to convince American troops that they were righteously battling monsters rather than fighting and killing other humans.

On the other hand, using loaded language to elicit a positive reaction from listeners often occurs in politics. When politicians want to raise taxes to pay for various programs and services, they often avoid terms such as "public spending" or "increased taxes." Instead, they prefer statements like "investment in public services," as this term has a more positive connotation. Using this positively loaded language, politicians are more likely to get support from the public, who often resist paying more for government programs and services.

Lecture Notes

Main Idea: _loaded lang. → appeal to emo._

Subtopic 1: _war_

Details: • _U.S. prop. → German "monsters"_

• _justify killing enemy (good vs. evil)_

Subtopic 2: _pol. → tax increases_

Details: • _tax ↑ = "invest. in public service"_

• _trick ppl. into gov. support_

Task 6

Model Answer

Question 6 of 6

Using information from the lecture, describe loaded language and summarize the two uses of loaded language discussed in the lecture.

 Response

The professor discusses loaded language, which is the use of words that appeal to people's emotions to rally support for a cause or criticize another group. He talks about the uses of loaded language during wars and in politics. To start, the lecturer talks about how Americans used loaded language to dehumanize German troops during World War II. For instance, American propaganda called German soldiers "monsters" and "brutes," encouraging Americans to think that they were fighting creatures rather than humans. Additionally, the professor discusses how politicians use loaded language to make tax increases seem more acceptable. For example, a politician may say that he's increasing "investments in public services" rather than saying that he's "increasing taxes." This strategy makes people feel that they're making an investment rather than just giving more money to the government in the form of taxes.

Now practice saying your response aloud. If possible, have a friend/classmate fill out this checklist as you say your response to him or her. If you are by yourself, record and listen to your response, and then fill out the checklist below on your own.

Deliver your response within 60 seconds.

Task 6 Response Checklist

	Yes	Somewhat	No
• Does the speaker briefly describe the main concept of the lecture?			
• Does the speaker summarize the two examples/topics that elaborate on the lecture's main concepts?			
• Does the speaker explain how these two examples/topics relate to one another?			
• Does the speaker deliver an organized response by using transition words and proper sentence structures?			
• Does the speaker deliver a coherent response by using appropriate tone and pronunciation?			
• Does the speaker finish within the time limit?			

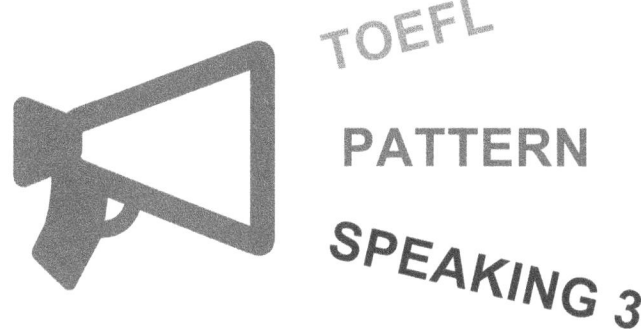

CHAPTER 7

Actual Practice

TOEFL iBT Independent Speaking Task Rubric (Tasks 1-2)

4	**OVERVIEW** - *Although the response may include brief lapses* in clarity, the vast majority of the response is intelligible and comprehensive. For a response to receive a score of 4, it must accomplish all of the following:* **SPEECH** - The speaker delivers an articulate response that requires little to no interpretation on the part of the listener. Any mistakes or omissions do not affect the listener's ability to comprehend the speaker's response. **VOCABULARY AND GRAMMAR** - The speaker demonstrates his or her command of a sophisticated vocabulary and an understanding of various sentence structures. Minimal pauses indicate a strong familiarity with the English language. Any vocabulary or grammar mistakes do not affect the listener's ability to understand the response. **CONTENT** - The speaker completely addresses all aspects of the prompt by presenting ideas in a logical and organized manner.
3	**OVERVIEW** - *The response may contain noticeable lapses in clarity and organization, but it is still consistently intelligible and exhibits a clear understanding of the prompt. for a response to receive a score of 3, it must accomplish at least two of the following:* **SPEECH** - The speaker delivers a response that is generally comprehensible, but noticeable pronunciation or inflection issues may occasionally obscure the speaker's meaning. **VOCABULARY AND GRAMMAR** - Although the speaker's grasp of vocabulary and grammar structures may be somewhat limited and occasionally inaccurate, any errors or mistakes do not greatly interfere with the speaker's overall ability to respond to the prompt. **CONTENT** - The speaker addresses all aspects of the prompt, even though the response may lack detailed explanations and may contain lapses in organization.

***Lapse**: a temporary decline in quality of something

2

OVERVIEW
- *The response includes information relevant to the prompt, but the listener's comprehension is hindered by frequent lapses in the speaker's fluency. For a response to receive a score of 2, it must accomplish at least two of the following:*

SPEECH
- The speaker delivers a response that requires active interpretation on the part of the listener. Although most of the response is intelligible, frequent pronunciation and inflection issues obscure the speaker's meaning.

VOCABULARY AND GRAMMAR
- A limited grasp of vocabulary and grammar structures often prevents the speaker from fully articulating his or her thoughts. The response is dominated by short, simple sentences and is characterized by a limited vocabulary.

CONTENT
- The response generally connects to the prompt, but it lacks details and examples. The few details and examples that are presented may be unclear or redundant.

1

OVERVIEW
- *The response barely addresses the prompt, and/or the majority of the response is incomprehensible. For a response to receive a score of 1, it must accomplish at least two of the following:*

SPEECH
- Frequent and reoccurring pronunciation and inflection issues make most of the response difficult to understand, if not entirely incomprehensible. Constant interpretation is required on the part of the listener.

VOCABULARY AND GRAMMAR
- A limited grasp of vocabulary and grammar prevents the speaker from articulating his or her thoughts. The speaker may rely heavily on clichés or memorized phrases and expressions.

CONTENT
- The speaker conveys little information that is relevant to the prompt. Only simple ideas are presented, and these ideas may be unclear or redundant.

0

OVERVIEW
- *The speaker does not respond to the prompt. The speaker may deliver a response that is unrelated to the prompt, or the speaker may deliver a response in a language other than English.*

TOEFL iBT Integrated Speaking Task Rubric (Tasks 3-6)

4

OVERVIEW
- *The speaker addresses all aspects of the prompt. Despite infrequent lapses in clarity, the response is intelligible and comprehensive. For a response to a receive a score of 4, it must address all of the following:*

SPEECH
- The speaker may pause in order to recall or reference information, but these pauses do not affect the listener's comprehension. Similarly, any mistakes or omissions do not affect the listener's ability to comprehend the speaker's response.

VOCABULARY AND GRAMMAR
- The speaker demonstrates his or her command of a sophisticated vocabulary and an understanding of various sentence structures. Minimal pauses indicate a strong familiarity with the English language. Any vocabulary or grammar mistakes do not affect the listener's ability to understand the response. The speaker uses nearly all relevant terms from the listening and/or reading portions of the task.

CONTENT
- The speaker organizes and presents nearly all relevant information presented in the task. The relationships between ideas are consistently clear.

3

OVERVIEW
- *The response may contain noticeable lapses in clarity and organization, but it is still consistently intelligible and exhibits a clear understanding of the requirements of the task. For a response to receive a score of 3, it must accomplish at least two of the following:*

SPEECH
- The speaker delivers a response that is generally comprehensible, but noticeable pronunciation or inflection issues may occasionally interfere with the speaker's ability to convey information presented in the task.

VOCABULARY AND GRAMMAR
- Although the speaker's grasp of vocabulary and grammar structures may be somewhat limited and occasionally inaccurate, any errors or mistakes do not greatly interfere with the speaker's overall ability to form a response. The speaker uses some relevant terms from the listening and/or reading portions of the task.

CONTENT
- The speaker addresses most of the relevant information presented in the task, but the response may be missing some details, contain some inaccurate information, or include lapses in organization and clarity.

2	**OVERVIEW** • *The response includes information relevant to the task, but some information may be inaccurate or omitted altogether. A lack of clarity or intelligibility may interfere with the listener's comprehension of the response. For a response to receive a score of 2, it must accomplish at least two of the following:* **SPEECH** • The speaker delivers a response that requires active interpretation on the part of the listener. Although most of the response is intelligible, frequent pronunciation and inflection issues obscure the speaker's meaning. **VOCABULARY AND GRAMMAR** • A limited grasp of vocabulary and grammar structures often prevent the speaker from fully articulating his or her thoughts. The response is dominated by short, simple sentences and is characterized by a limited vocabulary. The speaker uses few relevant terms from the listening and/or reading portions of the task. **CONTENT** • The response relates to the information presented in the task, but it contains many obvious omissions or inaccuracies. Any main ideas are explained vaguely or inaccurately, and main ideas may be confused with minor details or irrelevant information presented in the listening and/or reading portions of the task.
1	**OVERVIEW** • *The response includes very few pieces of information that are relevant to the task, and/or the majority of the response is incomprehensible. For a response to receive a score of 1, it must accomplish at least two of the following:* **SPEECH** • Frequent and reoccurring pronunciation and inflection issues make most of the response difficult to understand, if not entirely incomprehensible. Constant interpretation is required on the part of the listener. **VOCABULARY AND GRAMMAR** • A limited grasp of vocabulary and grammar prevents the speaker from articulating his or her thoughts. The speaker may rely heavily on clichés or memorized phrases and expressions. The speaker does not use any relevant terms from the listening and/or reading portions of the task. **CONTENT** • The speaker conveys little information that is relevant to the information presented in the task. Only simple ideas are presented, and these ideas may be unclear or redundant.
0	**OVERVIEW** • *The speaker does not respond to the prompt. The speaker may deliver a response that is unrelated to the prompt, or the speaker may deliver a response in a language other than English.*

Task 1

Question 1 of 6

What factors do you consider when you choose a restaurant? Explain why you take these factors into consideration. Please include specific examples and details in your explanation.

Preparation Time 00:00:15
Response Time 00:00:45

Notes

Response

TASK 2

Question 2 of 6

Some people like reading books while others like watching movies. Which pastime do you prefer and why? Support your answer with reasons.

Preparation Time 00:00:15
Response Time 00:00:45

Notes

Response

TASK 1

Model Answer

Question 1 of 6

What factors do you consider when you choose a restaurant? Explain why you take these factors into consideration. Please include specific examples and details in your explanation.

Notes

quality & service

1) quality of food
- rarely dine out
- quality + unique taste

2) service
- well-trained waiter → go again
- rude → never return

 Response

The factors that I always keep in mind when choosing a restaurant are the quality of the food and the service. Because I rarely go out to eat, I treat each trip to a restaurant like a treat. Therefore, I don't worry about price, and instead I focus on finding restaurants that offer high-quality food that tastes great. After all, nothing is better than finding a restaurant that uses quality ingredients to create a delicious, unique dish. The second most important thing is the service at the restaurant. Well-trained waiters make me feel comfortable, and that makes me want to return to the same restaurant again and again. I never want to go to a restaurant where the waiters are rude.

TASK 2

Model Answer

Question 2 of 6

Some people like reading books while others like watching movies. Which pastime do you prefer and why? Support your answer with reasons.

Notes

books

1) book
- no limit imagination
- diff. interpretation

2) movie
- no imagination → audience just follows along
- disappointing when movie is based on book

 Response

Given the choice between reading a book and watching a movie, I'll usually choose to read a book for a number of reasons. For one thing, reading books doesn't limit the reader's imagination like watching a movie does. Readers must use their imagination when envisioning a novel's scenery, a character's looks, or a story's events. As a result, everybody can have different views when it comes to interpreting the story. However, when watching a movie, people don't have the chance to imagine every situation. People just follow along with what the movie is showing. I think that's why most people feel disappointed when they see a movie that's based on a book: the way the book's characters and settings are represented on film is never exactly how the audience imagines it.

Question 3 of 6

⏱ Reading Time 00:00:45

Smith University to Vote on Changing Grading Methods

Next month, students will have the opportunity to vote on a new grading method. The university is considering changing from the traditional A through F letter-grade system to written evaluations. If students vote to change the grading method, all final report cards will be issued as a series of written evaluations, without A, B, C, D, or F letter grades. There are a couple of reasons for this. First, since this is a liberal, private university, many students favor the more comprehensive feedback of a written evaluation. Additionally, a recent large-scale study revealed that students who received written evaluations learned material better than those who received letter grades.

Announcement Notes

Now, listen to two students discuss the proposal.

Question 3 of 6

Conversation Notes

Question 3 of 6

The man expresses his opinion regarding the proposed written evaluation system. Briefly summarize the proposal, state his opinion the reasons he gives for holding this opinion.

Preparation Time 00:00:30
Response Time 00:01:00

Response

TASK 3

Model Answer

Question 3 of 6

⏲ Reading Time 00:00:45

Smith University to Vote on Changing Grading Methods

Next month, students will have the opportunity to vote on a new grading method. The university is considering changing from the traditional A through F letter-grade system to written evaluations. If students vote to change the grading method, all final report cards will be issued as a series of written evaluations, without A, B, C, D, or F letter grades. There are a couple of reasons for this. First, since this is a liberal, private university, many students favor the more comprehensive feedback of a written evaluation. Additionally, a recent large-scale study revealed that students who received written evaluations learned material better than those who received letter grades.

Announcement Notes

proposal: change, letter grades → writ. eval.

reasons: 1) stud. favor more comprehensive feedback   2) study → stud. learn better

---

Now, listen to two students discuss the proposal.

F: What do you think of this proposal to change the grading system?
M: In theory, I favor the idea. But in practice, I don't think the new system will work.
F: What do you mean?
M: First of all, think about how impractical this written evaluation system will be with subjects like math, engineering, and computer programming.
F: You know, I hadn't thought of that.
M: With those subjects, you either understand the material or you don't, so letter grades are a better way to evaluate a student's skill in those classes.
F: I have to agree with you there.
M: In addition, I think the written evaluations are going to hurt us when we look for jobs after graduating.
F: How so?
M: Employers don't have time to read years of written evaluations. They need something quick, like a letter grade, to compare us with other possible candidates.
F: I guess so.
M: And anyway, employers are accustomed to letter grades, so I'm voting against the proposal.

F: Female Student / **M:** Male Student

Conversation Notes

man opposes

1) impractical → math, engi, comp. progress   2) bad for future employment

   • understand/don't → letter better   • bosses = no time to read evals.

                                                                                                                         • used to letter grades

Question 3 of 6

The man expresses his opinion regarding the proposed written evaluation system. Briefly summarize the proposal, state his opinion the reasons he gives for holding this opinion.

 Response

The university will allow students to decide whether they would prefer written evaluations to letter grades. The man doesn't believe it's a good idea to implement this change for a couple of reasons. First, he says that written evaluations are impractical for classes that contain objective material, such as math, engineering, and computer programming. Letter grades are the only way to prove that a student understands the major concepts in these classes. Second, he says that written evaluations are impractical for future employment. According to him, employers don't have the time to read every student evaluation. Also, employers aren't accustomed to written evaluations, implying that they might make a negative impression when a student is looking for employment.

Task 4

Question 4 of 6

⏱ Reading Time 00:00:45

Shaky Camera Technique

The shaky camera technique is a type of film shooting done with a handheld camera. When this technique is used, the audience receives a first-person perspective of the action occurring in the film. Many film directors use this technique today when they want their audiences to feel an unfiltered sense of reality along with nervousness, immersion, and dynamism. The shaky camera technique is popular in documentary filmmaking and in movies where first-hand experiences are emphasized.

Passage Notes

_____

_____

Now listen to part of a lecture in a film studies class.

Question 4 of 6

Lecture Notes

___

Question 4 of 6

The professor talks about shaky camera technique. Use the examples from the lecture to describe the shaky camera technique and summarize its uses in filmmaking.

Preparation Time 00:00:30
Response Time   00:01:00

Response

Task 4

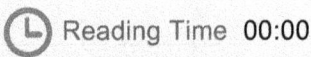

Question 4 of 6

Reading Time 00:00:45

Shaky Camera Technique

The shaky camera technique is a type of film shooting done with a handheld camera. When this technique is used, the audience receives a first-person perspective of the action occurring in the film. Many film directors use this technique today when they want their audiences to feel an unfiltered sense of reality along with nervousness, immersion, and dynamism. The shaky camera technique is popular in documentary filmmaking and in movies where first-hand experiences are emphasized.

Passage Notes

shaky cam. tech.
* *first-person perspective*

Now listen to part of a lecture in a film studies class.

Sometimes, film directors want their audiences to feel as if they're watching or having a real-life experience. To accomplish this, directors will often use the shaky camera technique, which has been popular since the 1960s. Let me give you two examples of the shaky camera technique.

First, let's look at the 1998 Steven Spielberg film Saving Private Ryan. This film opens with the 1944 World War II Allied assault of Omaha Beach, France. The entire opening sequence, where North American and European troops "storm the beach," is shot using the shaky camera technique. This technique emphasized the intensity and violence of war. The shaky cameras follow the troops from the boats to the beach and inland. Because of this filming technique, viewers feel like they're traveling with the troops as they endure the terror and confusion of battle.

Next, let's discuss at the 1999 horror film The Blair Witch Project. This entire film is shot using the shaky camera technique. The film appears to be an amateur documentary in which student filmmakers are searching for a witch in the woods of Maryland. However, the movie is actually a horror film that uses the shaky camera technique to lend a feeling of amateurism and realism to the film. Because of this technique, audiences feel like they're right next to the actors, trapped in the dark woods and surrounded by a mysterious force.

Lecture Notes

1) Saving Private Ryan	2) The Blair Witch Project
• opening, beach battle → shaky cam	• all shaky cam.
• emphasize w/ soldiers → intensity, war	• search for a witch, horror film
• realism, immersion	• create audience fear

Question 4 of 6

The professor talks about shaky camera technique. Use the examples from the lecture to describe the shaky camera technique and summarize its uses in filmmaking.

 Response

The shaky camera technique is a way of shooting a movie that creates a sense of realism and immersion. The lecture gives two examples to illuminate the technique. First, the professor talks about a film called *Saving Private Ryan*. The shaky camera technique is used during the first scene, where troops storm Omaha Beach in France. By using this technique, the director makes the audience feel as if they're right besides the charging soldiers, experiencing the terror of war. Next, the professor talks about the film *The Blair Witch Project*, which is a horror film about a search for a witch. The entire film was shot using the shaky camera technique. With this technique, the movie seems like a documentary rather than a fictional film, and this sense of realism keeps audiences feeling scared throughout the film.

Task 5

Listen to the conversation between a student and an advisor.

Question 5 of 6

Conversation Notes

Preparation Notes

Question 5 of 6

The people discuss two solutions to the man's problem. Describe the problem, explain how the student should solve his problem, and provide reasons that support your solution.

Preparation Time 00:00:20
Response Time 00:01:00

Response

Task 5

Model Answer

Listen to the conversation between a student and an advisor.

MS: Hello. I'd like to enroll for the fall semester.

A: Alright, sir. Let me just see your enrollment form. (Looks at form.) Uh, sir? There seems to be a problem. You've enrolled in an upper division Spanish class, and you need to take the introductory classes first.

MS: Oh, but I'm already pretty fluent. You see, my dad is from Spain and —

A: I'm afraid that doesn't matter. The rules say that you have to complete Spanish 1, 2 and 3 before you take Advanced Spanish.

MS: But that's ridiculous. I can already speak at a high level. Can't I do something to get in?

A: Well, why don't you just start from the beginning? You know, doing so might actually be a good idea because you can excel in the class.

MS: Well, yeah, but is there any way I can get in the advanced class this semester?

A: Well, the Spanish department does offer an exam for students, which allows them to "test out" of certain classes. This means you take the test, and if you pass, you don't have to take first three levels of Spanish. Fortunately for you, the exams are only administered during summer.

MS: Oh, so I could take the test before school starts?

A: Yes. That means you might be able to take the test before school starts in September, as it's only July right now.

MS: Male Student / **A:** Advisor

Conversation Notes

problem: can't take upper Spanish

sol. 1: start from the beginning

sol. 2: exam to test out classes

Preparation Notes

exam to test out classes before school starts

if pass → no intro. classes

- waste time if take intro. classes

- fair, prove his ability

Question 5 of 6

The people discuss two solutions to the man's problem. Describe the problem, explain how the student should solve his problem, and provide reasons that support your solution.

 Response

The student's problem is that he has to take introductory classes before he enrolls in the Advanced Spanish class. Since the man is already fluent in Spanish, he feels that he's ready to take a high level Spanish class. The advisor suggests that he either start from the beginning of the Spanish class series or take an exam that could replace the introductory classes. I definitely think he should pursue the second option. If he takes those introductory classes, he might get good grades, but it'll waste much of his precious time. Moreover, he'll probably find that taking a class that covers familiar material will be boring. Plus, I think taking the exam is a reasonable way for him to prove his ability. Since he can take the test before the school year starts, there won't be any problems once he passes the test, and he won't waste his time going over familiar material in an easy Spanish class for an entire year.

Task 6

Now listen to part of a lecture in an education class.

Question 6 of 6

Lecture Notes

Question 6 of 6

The professor discusses academic freedom in the lecture. Describe academic freedom and explain how it has been challenged in the past.

Preparation Time 00:00:20
Response Time 00:01:00

Response

TASK 6

Model Answer

Now listen to part of a lecture in an education class.

Today I want to talk about an important right possessed by students and professors at Western universities and colleges. It's called academic freedom. For professors, academic freedom is the right to teach and conduct research without fear of punishment. For students, academic freedom is the right to challenge their teachers without fear of punishment. The idea behind academic freedom is that civilization benefits from academic discoveries, which are often made by challenging pre-existing systems or beliefs. However, academic freedom has been attacked and challenged many times. I'd like to share two such challenges right now—one by religion and the other by government.

The first attack came when the idea of academic freedom was just starting in Europe during the 1200s. At that time, the Catholic Church oversaw the creation of many universities throughout Europe. Teachers at universities wanted freedom to study any subject. However, the church persecuted many teachers whose ideas went against religious dogma. One teacher who challenged religious dogma under the cover of academic freedom was the Italian scientist Galileo. In the 1600s, the church persecuted Galileo for supporting the idea that the Earth moves around the Sun, which contradicted the traditional church teachings that the Earth was the center of the universe.

Another famous challenge to academic freedom came in the United States after World War II ended. At that time, government officials attacked academic freedom in American universities because they believed that there were a large number of Communist instructors. This fear led to investigations of professors at several universities by the U.S. House of Representatives. As a result, several professors were unfairly charged with being Communists and lost their jobs. Few Communists were found, but the investigation caused many Americans to fear that universities were full of Communists.

Lecture Notes

acad. freedom → speak w/o fear of punish

1) Catholic Church

  • attack if against beliefs

  • Galileo, heliocentric

2) U.S. gov.

  • after WW2, communists investigated @ univ.

   → few comm., but teachers lost jobs

Question 6 of 6

The professor discusses academic freedom in the lecture. Describe academic freedom and explain how it has been challenged in the past.

 Response

Academic freedom is the freedom to express one's ideas in an academic setting without fear of punishment. In the lecture, the professor talks about situations in which religious and government organizations challenged academic freedom. First, the professor discusses a time when the Catholic church challenged academic freedom. During the Medieval period, the church would try to silence any ideas that challenged the church's dogma. Thus, when Galileo claimed that the Earth moves around the Sun, the church rejected his claims, denying him academic freedom. Next, the professor says that academic freedom was challenged after World War II in the U.S. At that time, the U.S. government believed that many Communists were teaching at American universities. As a result, some professors were harassed by the government. Ultimately, some professors even lost their jobs because they were wrongly accused of being Communists.

Task 1

Question 1 of 6

What is your favorite subject in school? Explain why this subject is your favorite. Include examples to support your answer.

Preparation Time 00:00:15
Response Time 00:00:45

Notes

Response

TASK 2

Question 2 of 6

Some people prefer to go to bed early and wake up early. Others prefer to go to bed late and wake up late. Which sleeping schedule do you prefer? Support your answer with reasons.

Preparation Time 00:00:15
Response Time 00:00:45

Notes

Response

Task 1

Model Answer

Question 1 of 6

What is your favorite subject in school? Explain why this subject is your favorite. Include examples to support your answer.

Notes

science

1) bio.
- dissections → learn function of internal organs

2) chem.
- element combos.
- mix chem. → result like magic

 Response

My favorite subject in school is science. I think science is very interesting because it requires students to conduct actual experiments and think about how the world around them functions. For example, in biology class, I think it's very interesting to dissect animals and see their internal organs. By doing so, I've come to realize how much all living creatures have in common with one another. And knowing about how body parts function is incredibly interesting, too. Additionally, in chemistry class, I think it's fascinating to learn about the ways that different elements can combine to form the incredibly diverse world that surrounds us. Also, I really like mixing different chemicals and solutions; it seems almost magical the way two dissimilar chemicals can interact with each other.

TASK 2

Model Answer

Question 2 of 6

Some people prefer to go to bed early and wake up early. Others prefer to go to bed late and wake up late. Which sleeping schedule do you prefer? Support your answer with reasons.

Notes

sleep late → wake up late

1) can't wake up early

　• not alert in am

　• no sleep early in pm

(2) like night time

　• focus on work → quiet

Response

Personally, I prefer to go to bed late at night and wake up late the next morning. Certainly, some statistics show that sleeping and waking up early is good for our health, but I just can't wake up early in the morning. No matter how much coffee I drink, I can't gather my senses in the early morning. And because I usually get up late in the morning, I can never fall asleep until late at night. Moreover, I like staying awake until late at night because I can focus on my work better at this time. Since many people are sleeping at night, it's very quiet and still, making perfect conditions for me to work.

Task 3

Question 3 of 6

⏱ Reading Time 00:00:45

State University to Expand Library

Next year, State University is going to expand the size of its main library. There are two reasons for this remodeling. First, the main library is fifty years old, and students frequently complain about the outdated equipment and old furniture. All the library facilities will be updated during the construction project. Second, the main library looks out of place compared to other modern buildings around it. Most of the buildings near the main library were built within the last ten years, so the main library needs a new architectural design to "fit in."

Announcement Notes

___

___

Now, listen to two students discuss the article.

Question 3 of 6

Conversation Notes

Question 3 of 6

The male student expresses opinion of the new library proposal. State his opinion and the reasons he gives for holding his opinion.

Preparation Time 00:00:30
Response Time 00:01:00

Response

Task 3

Question 3 of 6

⏱ Reading Time 00:00:45

State University to Expand Library

Next year, State University is going to expand the size of its main library. There are two reasons for this remodeling. First, the main library is fifty years old, and students frequently complain about the outdated equipment and old furniture. All the library facilities will be updated during the construction project. Second, the main library looks out of place compared to other modern buildings around it. Most of the buildings near the main library were built within the last ten years, so the main library needs a new architectural design to "fit in."

Announcement Notes

proposal: expand size of main library

reasons: 1) library old   2) looks out of place

Now, listen to two students discuss the article.

F: What do you think of this proposal to expand the main library?
M: Well, I think the university is making the wrong changes.
F: What do you mean?
M: To start, I don't think they need to "expand" the library to make the needed improvements. The school can make the architectural, design, and equipment improvements without expanding the library, after all.
F: That's true.
M: Besides, the land they're going to use to expand the library is the place where my friends and I study and eat lunch every day.
F: Oh, yeah. That is a nice spot—the place with the trees and grass.
M: Uh-huh.
F: But won't it be nice to have a larger main library?
M: Well, that's the other thing. I don't really use the main library very much.
F: You don't?
M: Not really, and neither do my friends. We are all science majors. There are two other libraries on campus that have better science materials.
F: I understand your point now.

F: Female Student / **M:** Male Student

Conversation Notes

man opposes

1) no need to expand
- improve w/o expand
- expand to study/eat area

2) not use main lib.
- sci. major
- 2 other lib. → sci. material

Question 3 of 6

The male student expresses opinion of the new library proposal. State his opinion and the reasons he gives for holding his opinion.

 Response

The university is planning to remodel and expand the campus' main library. The man doesn't think it's a good idea for the university to pursue this construction project. First, he says that he doesn't see a need for the expansion. The university can improve items like furniture and technological equipment without expanding. He also says that he and his friends like to study and eat in the area where the expansion will occur. Second, he says that science majors rarely use the main library. According to him, there are two other libraries more suited to his major. They have more materials for science classes. Apparently, the main library doesn't have a large amount of science-related material.

Task 4

Question 4 of 6

⏱ Reading Time 00:00:45

Umbrella Species

An *umbrella species* describes groups of plants or animals used by biologists to determine the overall health of the ecosystem in which these organisms live. Umbrella species are unusually sensitive to ecosystem and habitat changes. Thus, if a habitat or ecosystem is under stress, the umbrella species will show evidence of such stress. In effect, everything under the umbrella species is under stress if the species itself is in trouble. Umbrella species often cover large regions that include more than one type of habitat. Biologists believe that protecting an umbrella species may incidentally protect many other species within an ecosystem as well.

Passage Notes

_____

_____

Now listen to part of a lecture in a biology class.

Question 4 of 6

Lecture Notes

Question 4 of 6

The professor talks about the role of northern spotted owls in their habitat. Using information from the passage and the lecture, explain why northern spotted owls are considered an umbrella species.

Preparation Time 00:00:30
Response Time 00:01:00

Response

TASK 4

Question 4 of 6

⏱ Reading Time 00:00:45

Umbrella Species

An *umbrella species* describes groups of plants or animals used by biologists to determine the overall health of the ecosystem in which these organisms live. Umbrella species are unusually sensitive to ecosystem and habitat changes. Thus, if a habitat or ecosystem is under stress, the umbrella species will show evidence of such stress. In effect, everything under the umbrella species is under stress if the species itself is in trouble. Umbrella species often cover large regions that include more than one type of habitat. Biologists believe that protecting an umbrella species may incidentally protect many other species within an ecosystem as well.

Passage Notes

umbrella species

▪ *determine health of an ecosys.*   ▪ *sensitive to change*

Now listen to part of a lecture in a biology class.

To comprehend the concept of umbrella species, we need to look at a specific example.

In North America, an important umbrella species for the Pacific Northwest is the northern spotted owl. This owl prefers old-growth forests along the Pacific coast of northern California, Oregon, Washington, and British Columbia. The northern spotted owl does not adapt well to habitat disturbances. If the northern spotted owl is in decline, so are many other species that live "under" it.

Now, let's explore this concept in greater detail. First and foremost, a decline in the population of the northern spotted owl indicates the loss of old-growth forest habitat. When old-growth forests are reduced, dozens of other species that live under the canopy of the forest are threatened, too. These include several rodents and insects upon which northern spotted owls feed as well as numerous rare plants that depend on the forest's shade for protection.

Lecture Notes

1) N. America → northern spotted owl

- only old growth forests

- if owls decline → loss of OGF → species under canopy (rodent, insect, rare plant)

Question 4 of 6

The professor talks about the role of northern spotted owls in their habitat. Using information from the passage and the lecture, explain why northern spotted owls are considered an umbrella species.

 Response

An umbrella species is a species that's sensitive to environmental changes that scientists study in order to guage the overall health of an ecosystem. The lecture uses spotted owls found in North America as an example. According to the professor, the northern spotted owl lives in old growth forests found in the Pacific Northwest. This species of owl is very sensitive to changes in its habitat, so when the northern spotted owl's population declines, scientists know that that old growth forests in which the owl lives are stressed, too. Therefore, numerous species that live under the protection of the trees suffer as well, including rodents, insects and some rare plants.

Task 5

Listen to a conversation between two students.

Question 5 of 6

Conversation Notes

Preparation Notes

Question 5 of 6

In the conversation, the students discuss two possible solutions to the man's problem. Describe the problem, and then state which solution you prefer and why.

Preparation Time 00:00:20
Response Time 00:01:00

Response

Task 5

Model Answer

Listen to a conversation between two students.

F: Hey, Eric. Why haven't you been to any lectures for organic chemistry lately?

M: Oh, I dropped the class. It was just too hard for me. All they talked about was carbon, bonding, and compounds. It was just driving me crazy.

F: But you still want to be a physician, right?

M: Well, yeah.

F: Gosh, I can't believe you didn't talk to me about this.

M: Why, is there some way you could've helped me?

F: Of course. Not to brag or anything, but I'm actually really good at chemistry. I could've definitely helped you with your studies. In fact, if you want to try to re-enroll, I think I can help you with any problems you're having.

M: Re-enroll? The quarter is already half finished; I don't think I can do that. And even with your help, I don't feel like I can pass this class.

F: Well, you can definitely re-enroll. But whether or not you accept my help is up to you. Also, the university has an excellent tutoring center. You might want to get some help there, and then re-enroll in organic chemistry next year.

M: Right. That way I'll be better prepared. That sounds like a good option.

F: The only thing is you'd be behind the rest of the pre-med group in your classes then. But I suppose that's really not such a big deal.

F: Female Student / **M:** Male Student

Conversation Notes

problem: man dropped chem class, too hard

sol. 1: re-enroll now & get help from woman

sol. 2: get help from tutoring center & re-enroll next yr.

Preparation Notes

get help from tutoring center & re-enroll next yr.

not much time to catch up

→ may be too stressful & disastrous for man

being prepared more important

Question 5 of 6

In the conversation, the students discuss two possible solutions to the man's problem. Describe the problem, and then state which solution you prefer and why.

 Response

The man's problem is that he dropped his organic chemistry class because it was too difficult for him. To solve this problem, the woman gives two suggestions: re-enroll right away and get the woman's help, or use the tutoring center and then re-enroll next year. I think the man should get help at the tutoring center and re-enroll in the class next year. First, the class is half finished and there's not much time for the man to catch up on what he's missed. Also, the man says that he's not sure if he can do better even with the woman's help. So re-enrolling right now might be too stressful and disastrous for him. Furthermore, the fact that he'll be behind the other pre-med students is not a big deal. In my opinion, being better prepared in chemistry is more important for him.

Task 6

Now listen to part of a lecture in a biology class.

Question 6 of 6

Lecture Notes

Question 6 of 6

The professor discusses how fungi consume food. Describe how fungi "eat" and explain how the process is both helpful and harmful to humans.

Preparation Time 00:00:20
Response Time 00:01:00

Response

TASK 6

Model Answer

Now listen to part of a lecture in a biology class.

The fungal kingdom includes many species of molds and mushrooms that have dramatic effects on their surroundings. In many ways, fungi support life as we know it; but at the same time, some fungi are extremely harmful. Today, let's explore one reason that fungi have such profoundly different impacts on the world: the way they consume food.

Fungi aren't plants, so they can't derive energy from sunlight. They "eat" other life forms, such as dead leaves. But they're not animals, either, and they don't have body structures such as stomachs for digesting. So how do they eat? Essentially, the fungi process their food outside of their bodies. They secrete acids and enzymes onto their food, which break it down, and then they absorb it like a sponge. By digesting food outside of their bodies, they're largely responsible for recycling organic wastes and freeing up nutrients in the soil. As a result, they make plant life, and by extension human life, possible here on Earth.

Now, as crucial as fungi are to life on Earth, they also can do their fair share of harm when they set out to decompose organic matter such as our homes, our food, or even ourselves. Remember that fungi "digest" matter by releasing chemicals into their surroundings. The digestive chemicals as well as other toxins or spores that the fungi produce can be extremely harmful to other organisms. The harmful products can contaminate crops or stores of grains, fruits, and vegetables, can kill animals, and can cause disease or severe allergic reactions in people. Thus, fungi can be highly destructive.

Lecture Notes

fungi: how they eat → helpful/harmful

1) eat → helpful

  • release acid/enzyme → break down food (dead organisms)

  • break-down process → release nutrients into earth, recycle = beneficial

2) eat → harmful

  • harmful toxins → digestion

  • harm crops, kill animals, allergen

Question 6 of 6

The professor discusses how fungi consume food. Describe how fungi "eat" and explain how the process is both helpful and harmful to humans.

 Response

The professor talks about fungi in the lecture. She talks about how fungi consume food, and how this process can be both beneficial and harmful to other living creatures. First, she discusses the ways fungi digestion can benefit us. According to the lecture, fungi eat by releasing enzymes and proteins that break down food, which is then absorbed into the fungus for nutrients. This process usually breaks down dead organisms, and doing so releases helpful nutrients into the earth. Thus, fungi recycle organisms when they eat. However, the way fungi digest food outside of their bodies can also be harmful to living creatures. Because the digestive proteins that fungi release can break down living and non-living things, they can destroy crops, harm animals, and cause allergic reactions in humans. Thus, these helpful proteins can also act as toxins.

Task 1

Question 1 of 6

Where would you like to spend your ideal vacation? Why would you choose this place over others? Give reasons and examples for your answer.

Preparation Time 00:00:15
Response Time 00:00:45

Notes

Response

TASK 2

Question 2 of 6

Some people prefer a career where they have to work primarily with their hands. Others prefer a career that requires mental exertion but little physical effort. Which do you prefer and why? Support your answer with specific reasons and details.

Preparation Time 00:00:15
Response Time 00:00:45

Notes

Response

TASK 1

Model Answer

Question 1 of 6

Where would you like to spend your ideal vacation? Why would you choose this place over others? Give reasons and examples for your answer.

Notes

ideal vacation = Greece

1) rich w/ culture & hist.

  • visit Athens → ancient ruins

2) beautiful geography & scenery

  • swim in Mediterranean

  • see Mt. Olympus

Response

If I could visit any location on Earth, I'd travel to Greece because of its rich history and beautiful scenery. For one, Greece has been inhabited for thousands of years, and it's considered the birthplace of Western civilization. Thus, there are many ancient ruins and long-lived cultural traditions that I'd like to experience. For instance, I've always dreamed of visiting the city of Athens so I could see the incredible ruins at the Acropolis. Additionally, Greece is made up of incredibly diverse geography. When visiting Greece, I'd love to swim in the Mediterranean's clear, blue waters. I'd also want to visit Mount Olympus, the tallest mountain in Greece and, according to Greek myths, the home of the Greek gods.

Task 2

Model Answer

Question 2 of 6

Some people prefer a career where they have to work primarily with their hands. Others prefer a career that requires mental exertion but little physical effort. Which do you prefer and why? Support your answer with specific reasons and details.

Notes

brain work

1) using hands → no talent

  • not good at art / arch. / machine

2) using brain → more interesting

  • ex) scholar

 Response

Although there are many benefits to working with one's hands, I prefer a job that mostly requires mental exertion. On the one hand, many jobs that require artisanship are usually related to art, architecture, or engineering. These kinds of jobs are interesting, but I don't have any artistic or mechanical talent. In fact, the one time I tried to change the oil in my car, I ended up doing more damage than good. Therefore, a life of handiwork is not for me. Moreover, I like jobs that require brain work because those jobs are more attractive. For example, whenever I see scholars studying or researching something, I can think of nothing else that I'd rather be doing. Everyone has a special talent, and I believe mine lies in academia and scholarship.

Task 3

Question 3 of 6

⏱ Reading Time 00:00:45

State University to Add New Graduation Requirement

Starting next year, all students must participate in a one-semester internship in order to graduate from State University. Internships will be in students' major area of study and will provide students with a "taste" of their future careers. These internships will require a minimum of 10 hours of commitment per week for the entire semester. Advisors will be available to assist students in their tasks. During the internship, students will work through a series of assignments in addition to writing a short research paper. A professor in the student's area of study will grade all assignments at the end of the internship, giving the student a "pass" or "no pass" mark.

Announcement Notes
_____
_____

Now listen to two students discuss the article.

Question 3 of 6

Conversation Notes

Question 3 of 6

The male student expresses his opinion regarding the information in the announcement. State his opinion and the reasons he gives for holding that opinion.

Preparation Time 00:00:30
Response Time 00:01:00

Response

TASK 3

Model Answer

Question 3 of 6

⏱ Reading Time 00:00:45

State University to Add New Graduation Requirement

Starting next year, all students must participate in a one-semester internship in order to graduate from State University. Internships will be in students' major area of study and will provide students with a "taste" of their future careers. These internships will require a minimum of 10 hours of commitment per week for the entire semester. Advisors will be available to assist students in their tasks. During the internship, students will work through a series of assignments in addition to writing a short research paper. A professor in the student's area of study will grade all assignments at the end of the internship, giving the student a "pass" or "no pass" mark.

Announcement Notes

proposal: internship requirement

_____

Now listen to two students discuss the article.

F: Did you read this article about the new internship requirement?
M: Yeah, I think it sounds horrible.
F: Really? How so?
M: Well, for one, think about our majors: you're a visual arts major, and I'm a music major. You want to paint for a living after graduating, and I want to play guitar in a rock band. What kind of internships are you and I going to get based on our prospective careers?
F: Yeah, I see where you're coming from. Neither of us has very practical careers planned out.
M: Oh, and another thing that bothers me about this whole internship thing is that, well, it's the end of our junior year, and I've taken most of my difficult classes. Next year, I was planning to take it easy. In fact, for my second semester, I was only going to take one class and spend the rest of my time playing music with my band.
F: Oh, that's too bad. Maybe they'll let you replace your internship with your participation in a band.
M: (Laughing) Ha-ha! Do you really think that the university is going to allow me to substitute my playing in a rock band for this internship experience? I seriously doubt it.
F: Yeah, you're probably right.

F: Female Student / **M:** Male Student

Conversation Notes

man opposes

1) man doesn't benefit   *2) disrupts plans*

  ▪ *music major*   ▪ ↑ *work*

                                     ▪ ↓ *band practice*

Question 3 of 6

The male student expresses his opinion regarding the information in the announcement. State his opinion and the reasons he gives for holding that opinion.

 Response

The man is opposed to the new semester-long internship graduation requirement for a couple of reasons. First, he claims that he doesn't have a major that benefits from the internship requirement. As a music major with plans to become a guitarist, there aren't many relevant internships that the university could offer. Second, the timing of the internship requirement upsets him. Because it's the end of his junior year, he had planned on having an easy schedule next year. He had planned to take only one class his second semester and use the free time to play in his band. Now his plan is ruined and he'll have to spend his time working on his internship instead.

Task 4

Question 4 of 6

⏲ Reading Time 00:00:45

Family Names from Britain

As in the rest of Europe, in Britain family names often originated as descriptors of particular ancestors. Centuries ago, English villagers might have distinguished between two neighbors with the same given name by calling one "Henry the Older" and the other "Henry the Younger," shortened later to just Henry Old or Henry Young. Family names such as "White" and "Black" probably referred to blond and brown hair color. "Armstrong" referred to strong arms. "Shakespeare" referred to someone's tendency to shake a spear. In the 13th and 14th centuries, such identifiers sometimes developed into *clan*, or family, names.

Passage Notes

_____
_____

Now, listen to a lecture on the topic in a linguistics class.

Question 4 of 6

Lecture Notes

Question 4 of 6

The professor talks about English-language family names. Use the examples from the lecture to explain how some of today's family names originated.

Preparation Time 00:00:30
Response Time 00:01:00

Response

TASK 4

Model Answer

Question 4 of 6

⏱ Reading Time 00:00:45

Family Names from Britain

As in the rest of Europe, in Britain family names often originated as descriptors of particular ancestors. Centuries ago, English villagers might have distinguished between two neighbors with the same given name by calling one "Henry the Older" and the other "Henry the Younger," shortened later to just Henry Old or Henry Young. Family names such as "White" and "Black" probably referred to blond and brown hair color. "Armstrong" referred to strong arms. "Shakespeare" referred to someone's tendency to shake a spear. In the 13th and 14th centuries, such identifiers sometimes developed into *clan*, or family, names.

Passage Notes

evolution of fam. names 13th, 14th c.

_____

Now, listen to a lecture on the topic in a linguistics class.

Even today, not all cultures use family names, and in Britain, they were only slowly adopted over time. At first, they were just identifiers of individuals. They were sometimes personal features, as we have seen, or they may have referred to a person's occupation or parentage.

In English, job titles often end in "-er," such as "Baker." A person who transported goods by cart would've been a "Carter." A "Potter" would've been someone who made ceramic pots. Perhaps the most common English family name, "Smith," once described someone who worked with metal, such as a blacksmith. The word "smith" comes from the verb "smite," meaning "strike," as a smith shapes hot metal by hitting it with a hammer.

Now, in communities where everyone knew everyone else, a boy or man could be distinguished by whose son he was. "Tim Jackson" would have meant Tim, Jack's son. "Mac" or "Mc" is a Scottish or Irish prefix meaning "son of," so "McDonald" would've meant Donald's son. The common name "Jones" is Welsh for John's son. By the 16th century, these names began to be legally fixed in written records and included all offspring in succeeding generations.

Lecture Notes

1) names related to occupation	2) names related to parent
• -er names, i.e. Baker, Potter	• Jackson = Jack's son
• Smith = "smite" = strike (metal)	• McDonald = Donald's son (Scottish, Irish)
• orig. 1 person's description	• Jones = John's son (Welsh)

Question 4 of 6

The professor talks about English-language family names. Use the examples from the lecture to explain how some of today's family names originated.

 Response

English-language family names began to develop in Britain in the 13th and 14th centuries, but they didn't start out as clan names. They were added to given names to help identify specific individuals through description. The lecture adds examples of two types of descriptions that became common family names: words that indicated either a person's job or parent. First, the lecturer explains that words with an –er at the end such as "baker" and "potter" became family names because they described a person by his job. The very common family name "Smith" is this type of name, as it refers to someone who works with, or "smites," metal. The lecturer also talks about family names that originally identified someone by whose son he was. This type of name ends in "son," such as "Jackson," or starts with "Mc" or "Mac," such as "McDonald." These common names first meant that an individual was "Jack's son" or "Donald's son."

Task 5

Listen to a conversation between two students.

Question 5 of 6

Conversation Notes

_____
_____
_____

Preparation Notes

Question 5 of 6

The students discuss two solutions to the man's problem. Describe the problem. Then state which solution you agree with and why.

Preparation Time 00:00:20
Response Time 00:01:00

Response

TASK 5

Model Answer

Listen to a conversation between two students.

F: Hey, Bob. What are you doing in the library so late on a Friday night?

M: Oh, my computer broke down, so I have to use the computers here. This is the only time that the library isn't packed.

F: Oh, I see. It seems so inconvenient. Why don't you just have your computer fixed?

M: Oh, uh, I'm pretty much out of money right now. I can barely afford to eat, if you know what I mean.

F: Gosh, that's terrible. Hey, I have an extra computer, if you'd like to borrow it.

M: Oh, thanks, but I don't want to inconvenience you.

F: It's no trouble at all, Bob. The only concern is—the computer is like seven years old. But it should be fine for word processing.

M: Well, thanks. Maybe I'll take you up on the offer.

F: Or, the school has this program where you can borrow a brand-new computer and pay for it at the end of the year. I was just reading about it.

M: Oh wow, like rent it for the year and then pay for it later. Hmm, that might be something to look into.

F: Female Student / M: Male Student

Conversation Notes

problem: man's comp. broken

sol. 1: borrow woman's old comp.

sol. 2: rent new comp. from school & pay later

Preparation Notes

- rent new comp. from school & pay later
- man doesn't want to inconvenience woman
- woman's comp. old
- more efficient & convenient

Question 5 of 6

The students discuss two solutions to the man's problem. Describe the problem. Then state which solution you agree with and why.

 Response

The man's problem is that he has to go to the library late at night to use its computers, as his is broken and he cannot afford to get it fixed. One solution to this problem is to borrow a computer from the woman, and the other solution is to rent a computer through a school program. I think the man should choose the second option. Although it'd be nice for the man to have free, unlimited access to a computer, as he would if he borrowed the woman's old computer, he says that he might feel like he's inconveniencing her. Moreover, the woman says that her computer is really old, so it might not work very well anyway. Additionally, he could take advantage of the school's program and use a new computer without having to pay for it immediately. With the brand new computer, he'd be able to complete all of his work more efficiently at his own convenience.

Task 6

Now listen to part of a lecture in a sociology class.

Question 6 of 6

Lecture Notes

_____
_____
_____
_____
_____
_____
_____

Question 6 of 6

Using points and examples from the talk, explain some of the similarities and differences between the two types of misconceptions presented by the professor.

Preparation Time 00:00:20
Response Time 00:01:00

Response

_____
_____
_____
_____
_____
_____
_____
_____
_____

Task 6

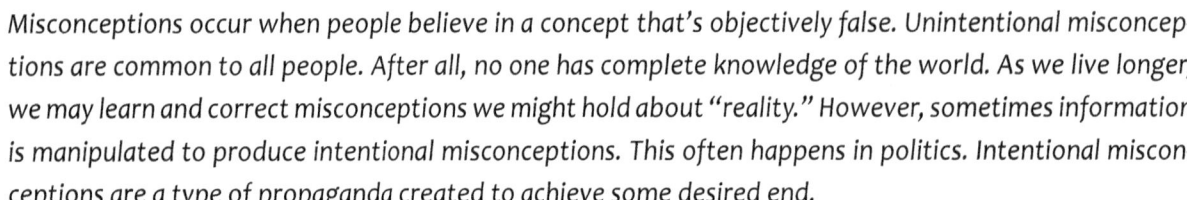

Now listen to part of a lecture in a sociology class.

Misconceptions occur when people believe in a concept that's objectively false. Unintentional misconceptions are common to all people. After all, no one has complete knowledge of the world. As we live longer, we may learn and correct misconceptions we might hold about "reality." However, sometimes information is manipulated to produce intentional misconceptions. This often happens in politics. Intentional misconceptions are a type of propaganda created to achieve some desired end.

Unintentional misconceptions are common in any subject lacking verifiable scientific research. For example, many Europeans during the Middle Ages believed the Sun revolved around Earth. This misconception was not perpetuated to promote any propaganda. It was merely based on their limited knowledge of the astronomy and physics. However, once the observations of astronomers such as Galileo Galilei disproved this misconception, people gradually dispelled their previous assumptions.

There are many instances of intentional misconceptions, especially in politics. For example, some American politicians overemphasized the threat of Communism during the 1950s and 1960s. They did this to scare people into voting for them; in order to defeat their opponents, these politicians created the misconception of a "Red Peril," which was implied as the imminent invasion of Communist forces into the U.S. Their opponents, who actually did not view communism in such dire terms, often lost elections as a result of the success of this political strategy.

Lecture Notes

misconceptions = believe in something false

1) unintentional
   - Middle Ages → Sun cirlces Earth (based on limited knowledge)
   - after sci. → misconception ↓

2) intentional
   - politics → overstate communist threat to scare, defeat opponents = successful strategy

Question 6 of 6

Using points and examples from the talk, explain some of the similarities and differences between the two types of misconceptions presented by the professor.

 Response

Misconceptions happen when one's belief in something is incorrect. The professor says that there are unintentional and intentional misconceptions. First, the professor describes an unintentional misconception held during the Middle Ages, when many Europeans thought that the Sun revolved around the Earth. They believed in this scientific misconception because they didn't have evidence proving it wrong. However, when scientists' experiments and observations proved that this belief was a misconception, many people changed their beliefs accordingly. Next, the professor describes an intentional misconception spread by some American politicians in the 1950s and 1960s. These American politicians overemphasized the threat of Communism to scare people and defeat their opponents. Because of the success of this strategy, many of these deceitful politicians won their elections.

Task 1

Question 1 of 6

Describe a time that you felt overwhelmed by a busy schedule. How did you cope with your feelings? Use specific examples or details in your answer.

Preparation Time 00:00:15
Response Time 00:00:45

Notes

Response

TASK 2

Question 2 of 6

Some people like to travel with a companion while other people prefer to travel alone. Which do you prefer and why? Support your answer with reasons.

Preparation Time 00:00:15
Response Time 00:00:45

Notes

Response

TASK 1

Model Answer

Question 1 of 6

Describe a time that you felt overwhelmed by a busy schedule. How did you cope with your feelings? Use specific examples or details in your answer.

Notes

senior yr. of high school → stressed

- too much to do → exams, school act., chores, college app., scholarship

1) wrote down sched. for the day
   - est. time to complete tasks
   - only 3 hrs. → calmer

 Response

There was a time in my life when I felt overwhelmed by my schedule. When I was in my last year of high school, I felt that I had to prepare for many exams, commit myself to after-school activities, do chores at home, and apply for colleges and scholarships. One day I even just put my head in my arms in class. My teacher pulled me to the side and asked me what was wrong. When I told her, she made me write down everything I had to do that day after school, and then estimate how much time each task would take. Once I did that, I saw that all my tasks combined would only take about three hours. That day I learned how to get a calmer perspective.

TASK 2

Model Answer

Question 2 of 6

Some people like to travel with a companion while other people prefer to travel alone. Which do you prefer and why? Support your answer with reasons.

Notes

alone

1) reflect → need quiet moment
   - travel w/ others → no quiet time
2) more friends
   - travel w/ companion → talk only w/ companion = can't make new friends
   - like meeting new ppl.

 Response

Given the options of traveling with a group or traveling alone, I'll always choose to travel alone for a couple of reasons. Personally, one of the reasons I travel is to have some time alone to reflect on my life. Since I normally live a very hectic life, I really need some peace and quiet from time to time. But when I travel with a companion, I'm not able to have this type of quality time alone. In addition, when traveling alone, I can make new friends. When I travel with a companion, that's usually the only person I talk to during the trip, which means I don't talk to strangers. And I find it very rewarding and interesting to meet people from different parts of the world, so I prefer to travel alone in order to meet these interesting people.

Task 3

Question 3 of 6

Reading Time 00:00:45

School to Expand Parking Lot

State University is going to double the size of its main parking lot next year. Currently, the parking lot does not meet the needs of the current student population, as there are not enough spaces for all students to park. Additionally, the parking lot is next to an empty grass area owned, but not being used, by the university. Thus, the university will not have to buy any additional land to make the expansion.

Announcement Notes

_____

_____

Now listen to two students speak about the article.

Question 3 of 6

Conversation Notes

Question 3 of 6

The male student expresses his opinion regarding the announcement. State his opinion and explain the reasons he gives for holding this opinion.

Preparation Time 00:00:30
Response Time 00:01:00

Response

TASK 3

Model Answer

Question 3 of 6

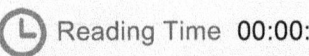 Reading Time 00:00:45

School to Expand Parking Lot

State University is going to double the size of its main parking lot next year. Currently, the parking lot does not meet the needs of the current student population, as there are not enough spaces for all students to park. Additionally, the parking lot is next to an empty grass area owned, but not being used, by the university. Thus, the university will not have to buy any additional land to make the expansion.

Announcement Notes

proposal: expand parking lot

reasons: 1) not enough parking space   2) univ.'s empty land = no extra $

Now listen to two students speak about the article.

F: Hey, did you read the article in the school paper about the new parking lot proposal?
M: Yeah, and I think it's a terrible idea. I mean, the logic the university uses for the expansion is flawed.
F: What do you mean?
M: For one, it's true that all students can't park in the main lot, but that doesn't really matter because many students park off campus to save money.
F: You mean in the "free" residential spaces nearby.
M: Exactly. So expanding the lot doesn't guarantee that all students will park there.
F: Well, I guess that's true. But what about in the future? The school is always growing, and they'll need more parking spaces for new students at some point.
M: Right, that's true. But they don't need to double the size of the lot. It takes decades for the school population to double.
F: Really?
M: Yeah. My dad went here thirty years ago, and the university still hasn't doubled its student population since then.

F: Female Student / **M:** Male Student

Conversation Notes

man opposes

1) students park off campus 2) no need to double size
  - save $ - stud. pop. slow
  - no need for new lot   - stud. pop. not doubled in 30 yrs.

Question 3 of 6

The male student expresses his opinion regarding the announcement. State his opinion and explain the reasons he gives for holding this opinion.

 Response

The man disagrees with the university's decision to double the size of the main parking lot. First, he says that not all students park in the main parking lot. Many students park off campus to save money. These students won't use the new lot, regardless of the expansion. Second, he says that the university doesn't need to double the size of the current lot. He believes that it takes a very long time for the university to double its student population. As an example, he points out that his father attended the university 30 years ago, and its student population hasn't doubled since then.

TASK 4

Question 4 of 6

 Reading Time 00:00:45

Doctrine of Signatures

In 16th-century Europe, people viewed plants much differently than they do today. Back then, Europeans believed in a philosophy called the "doctrine of signatures," which claimed that God made plants with a sign, or "signature," that showed their medicinal purpose in relationship to human beings. For Europeans of the time, it meant that plants were shaped like the human body parts for which they had useful purpose. In other words, they believed that a plant bearing parts that resembled human body parts had actual relevance to those parts.

Passage Notes

_____
_____

Now listen to part of a lecture on this topic in a botany class.

Question 4 of 6

Lecture Notes

Question 4 of 6

The professor describes two plants — lungwort and toothwort. Explain how these two plants illustrate the doctrine of signatures.

Preparation Time 00:00:30
Response Time 00:01:00

Response

TASK 4

Question 4 of 6

🕒 Reading Time 00:00:45

Doctrine of Signatures

In 16th-century Europe, people viewed plants much differently than they do today. Back then, Europeans believed in a philosophy called the "doctrine of signatures," which claimed that God made plants with a sign, or "signature," that showed their medicinal purpose in relationship to human beings. For Europeans of the time, it meant that plants were shaped like the human body parts for which they had useful purpose. In other words, they believed that a plant bearing parts that resembled human body parts had actual relevance to those parts.

Passage Notes

doctrine of signatures

• *God → plant shape = body part → med. purpose for that body part*

Now listen to part of a lecture on this topic in a botany class.

Now, let's discuss two examples that will help you better understand the "doctrine of signatures."

First, let's talk about Europeans' perceptions of a plant they called "lungwort." 16th-century European scientists believed that lungwort's oval-shaped leaves resembled diseased lungs. As a result, many doctors at this time used lungwort to treat coughs and respiratory infections. Although modern science has proven otherwise, some people still believe that lungwort has benefits in treating lung problems.

Next, there's a plant in the mustard family that 16th-century Europeans named toothwort. The name refers to the deeply cut lobes in the leaves, which resemble teeth. Of course, as the name implies, Europeans thought that by eating the leaves they could reduce pain in the mouth, from either toothache or other causes. While there's no medical evidence that toothwort has any effect on mouth pain, it's interesting to note that when Europeans came to North America, they saw that many Native American tribes chewed toothwort because they believed it had the same effects.

Lecture Notes

1) lungwort

- leaves = diseased-lung shape →
- cure cough, respiration
- modern med. disprove

2) toothwort

- leaves = teeth shape → ↓ mouth pain
- Native Am. use too

Question 4 of 6

The professor describes two plants—lungwort and toothwort. Explain how these two plants illustrate the doctrine of signatures.

 Response

The "doctrine of signatures" is based on the idea that plants that look like a certain body part can be used to cure that body part. In the lecture, the professor gives two examples of the doctrine of signatures. First, the professor describes a plant called lungwort. The leaves of this plant resemble diseased lungs. As a result, Europeans used the leaves to treat breathing problems. Interestingly, some modern people still believe that this plant can cure respiratory issues. Next, the professor describes a plant called toothwort. The leaves of toothwort have ridges that resemble teeth. As a result, Europeans chewed on the leaves of this plant to treat pain in the mouth. Coincidentally, Native Americans used the plant for the same purpose.

Task 5

Listen to a conversation between two students.

Question 5 of 6

Conversation Notes
_____
_____
_____

Preparation Notes

Question 5 of 6

The students discuss two solutions to the woman's problem. Describe her problem, and then state which solution you agree with and why.

Preparation Time 00:00:20
Response Time 00:01:00

Response

Task 5

Model Answer

Listen to a conversation between two students.

M: How did you do on that research paper you were so excited about?

F: I'm so disappointed. The professor gave me a "D."

M: No way! But you put so much hard work into that paper. Maybe he made a mistake.

F: I don't think so. He wrote a lot of notes on the paper explaining why he gave me the grade.

M: Hmm... Well, maybe you should talk to him about it. I mean, he might change your grade. You worked on that paper every day for nearly two months. Once he understands how much effort you put into it, I bet he'll go easy on you.

F: I don't think so. The professor is a pretty stubborn person, you know. He's very strict about his grading system.

M: Well, I still think it's worth a try.

F: Actually, he also said in his notes that I could rewrite the paper making the corrections he suggested.

M: Really? And then turn it in to be graded again?

F: Exactly. But I kind of think the paper is perfect the way it is. I don't want to make any changes.

M: I see. Well, you've got a tough decision on your hands.

M: Male Student / **F:** Female Student

Conversation Notes

problem: bad grade on research ppr.

sol. 1: talk to prof.

sol. 2: rewrite the ppr.

Preparation Notes

rewrite ppr. → must be a reason for bad grade

if prof. stubborn, talking won't change grade

be humble & follow prof.'s advice → higher chance for better grade

Question 5 of 6

The students discuss two solutions to the woman's problem. Describe her problem, and then state which solution you agree with and why.

 Response

The woman's problem is that she received a "D" on a research paper she put a lot of effort into. The students discussed two solutions: talk to the professor and persuade him to change the grade, or make the corrections and rewrite the paper. I agree with the latter idea, which is to rewrite the paper. Just because it took a lot of time to complete the paper doesn't mean that the paper is worth a good grade. Teachers don't give out grades at random, so there must be legitimate reasons she received the grade that she did. And besides, if the teacher is as stubborn as the woman claims, then talking to him won't earn her a better grade on the paper. In my opinion, even though she thinks her paper is perfect, she wouldn't have received a "D" for no reason. I believe she should change her stubborn attitude. She should be more humble and rewrite the paper, following the advice given by her professor.

Task 6

Now listen to part of a lecture in a biology class.

Question 6 of 6

Lecture Notes

Question 6 of 6

Using information from the lecture, explain the two purposes of bioluminescence presented by the professor.

Preparation Time 00:00:20
Response Time 00:01:00

Response

TASK 6

Model Answer

Now listen to part of a lecture in a biology class.

Today, I'd like to discuss bioluminescence. For those of you unfamiliar with the term, bioluminescence means "living light." It describes the ability of some living organisms to produce light within their bodies. Unlike the light produced by the sun, bioluminescence is produced by a cold chemical reaction. In other words, the light produced within the organisms is created completely by chemical interactions and generates little heat. Now I'm going to explain two purposes of bioluminescence so that you can better understand how it works. Often, organisms use bioluminescence for mating and illumination.

Perhaps the most commonly seen example of bioluminescence worldwide occurs in fireflies. Fireflies are a type of flying beetle that produces light using organs in its stomach area. When these insects fly at night, it appears that their abdomens are filled with a glowing green-yellow light. The main purpose of bioluminescence in these beetles appears to be finding a mate. Male fireflies' abdomens flash on and off during courtship. When a female is attracted to a male, she may flash in response, initiating the mating ritual.

Bioluminescence is also common among deep-sea animals. Many creatures that inhabit the deep sea have some type of bioluminescent capability, and some deep-sea creatures use their light ability for illumination. The deep sea is completely dark. As a result, many of the organisms there are blind. For those whose eyes do function, they may use bioluminescence to navigate their environment, seek out prey or mates, and defend territory.

Lecture Notes

bioluminescence

1) mating

   • *ex. firefly (beetle): cold light, stomach → green-yellow*

   • *males use → attract mate*

2) illumination

   • *deep-sea fish → can't see in dark*

   • *bioluminescence = defend, navigate, hunt*

Question 6 of 6

Using points and examples from the talk, explain the two purposes of bioluminescence presented by the professor.

 Response

Bioluminescence describes a type of light produced by some animals through "cold" chemical reactions. The professor explains two purposes of bioluminescence: mating and illumination. One purpose of bioluminescence is for finding mates. As an example, the professor talks about fireflies. These beetles produce a cold chemical reaction in their mid-sections that produces green-yellow light. The professor notes that the males may flash the lights off and on to attract females. Another purpose of bioluminescence is illumination. As an example, the professor talks about deep-sea creatures. Because their environment is very dark, some deep-sea animals are blind. But others use their bioluminescence for defending themselves, navigating, and hunting.

Task 1

Question 1 of 6

What are some ways that your own culture has shaped you? Use specific reasons and examples to support your answer.

Preparation Time 00:00:15
Response Time 00:00:45

Notes

Response

TASK 2

Question 2 of 6

Some people like to spend their free time outdoors while others like to spend their free time indoors. Which do you prefer and why? Support your answer with reasons.

Preparation Time 00:00:15
Response Time 00:00:45

Notes

Response

TASK 1

Model Answer

Question 1 of 6

What are some ways that your own culture has shaped you? Use specific reasons and examples to support your answer.

Notes

Confucian values

1) respect elders

2) elders 1st

 Response

My culture has shaped me in countless ways, especially through my parents' Confucian values. I was brought up to show nothing but respect to people who are older than me, and not to directly disagree with them. I've found that doing so sometimes makes me different from people who've been raised to always feel free to give their opinions. Another example is that in my culture, instead of "ladies first," we learn "elders first." I wait for an elder to do something first, such as to sit down or to begin eating. Also, I use special forms of language to show my respect to an elder. Of course, as I get older, I'll expect younger people to respect me. So Confucianism has helped shape my personality.

TASK 2

Model Answer

Question 2 of 6

Some people like to spend their free time outdoors while others like to spend their free time indoors. Which do you prefer and why? Support your answer with reasons.

Notes

outdoors

1) need sunlight

　　• study inside

2) activities

　　• health

　　• meet ppl.

 Response

Given the choice of spending my free time either indoors or outdoors, I definitely prefer spending my time outdoors. The first reason is that I need to get into the sunlight. Because I'm a student who's often writing essays and preparing for exams, I spend most of my time studying indoors. Going so many hours without sunlight makes me feel like I have cabin fever. So whenever possible, I try to go outside and get some sunlight. Often, just taking a walk around the block on a sunny day can greatly improve my mood. Also, I like outdoor activities such as hiking, playing tennis, and running. These things not only keep my body healthy, but they also give me a chance to meet people and enjoy life.

TASK 3

Question 3 of 6

🕒 Reading Time 00:00:45

Student Health Center to Improve Services

Starting next semester, the university's student health center is going to improve its services drastically. To start, the health center's current hours, Monday through Friday from 9:00 am to 6:00 pm, will be extended to 8:00 am to 8:00 pm. Additionally, the health center will now be open on Saturdays, from 10:00 am to 3:00 pm. Moreover, the center will begin offering additional services such as blood testing, eye examinations, and teeth cleaning. However, in order to obtain the group health insurance necessary to cover such services, the university will have to raise students' tuition by 150 dollars per year. The administration feels that this small cost will greatly benefit students.

Announcement Notes
_____
_____

Now listen to two students speak about the article.

Question 3 of 6

Conversation Notes

Question 3 of 6

The male student expresses his opinion about the announcement. State his opinion and explain the reasons he gives for holding this opinion.

Preparation Time 00:00:30
Response Time 00:01:00

Response

Task 3

Model Answer

Question 3 of 6

🕐 Reading Time 00:00:45

Student Health Center to Improve Services

Starting next semester, the university's student health center is going to improve its services drastically. To start, the health center's current hours, Monday through Friday from 9:00 am to 6:00 pm, will be extended to 8:00 am to 8:00 pm. Additionally, the health center will now be open on Saturdays, from 10:00 am to 3:00 pm. Moreover, the center will begin offering additional services such as blood testing, eye examinations, and teeth cleaning. However, in order to obtain the group health insurance necessary to cover such services, the university will have to raise students' tuition by 150 dollars per year. The administration feels that this small cost will greatly benefit students.

Announcement Notes

proposal: health center improve

- *↑ hrs. M-F, open on Sat., offer additional services*
- *↑ tuition by $150*

Now listen to two students speak about the article.

F: What do you think of the improved services that the administration is bringing to the student health center?

M: You know, initially I thought it sounded like a good idea. But the more I think about all these changes, the more I'm convinced that they're not beneficial, at least for me.

F: Really? You don't think paying 150 dollars a year for all those added services is a bargain?

M: Well, they'd be a bargain if I actually intended to use them, but I already have comprehensive health insurance under my parents' plan. I'm covered by their insurance until I'm 21 years old, so I don't really need to use the student health center until my last year in college. The health center is more for people who don't have any insurance.

F: I guess that's true. But the center is also for students who have emergencies on campus. The extended hours will be good for that.

M: But I don't live on campus anymore, so I don't really care about the extended hours. Plus, Central City Hospital is only a 5-minute drive from my apartment. If I need emergency treatment for anything, I'd probably go there.

F: I see. I guess that makes sense.

F: Female Student / M: Male Student

Conversation Notes

man disagrees

1) already have insurance
- no need for better health center

2) live off-campus
- go to hosp. instead
- $150 not worth for him

Question 3 of 6

The male student expresses his opinion about the announcement. State his opinion and explain the reasons he gives for holding this opinion.

 Response

The proposal states that the school will improve the health center by extending its hours and providing more health services. The man is opposed to the improvements being made to the student health center for a couple of personal reasons. First of all, the man claims that he already has comprehensive health insurance through his parents' plan. Therefore, he doesn't need to use the student health center to meet any of his health needs. Second, the extended health center hours won't benefit him because he lives in off-campus. He says that if an emergency occurred, he'd just go to the nearest hospital, which is 5 minutes away from his house. He believes that paying 150 dollars for services that he won't use is a waste.

TASK 4

Question 4 of 6

⏱ Reading Time 00:00:45

False Consensus Effect

In sociology, the *false consensus effect* describes the tendency for people to assume that others share their beliefs. Specifically, it describes the misconception in which you assume that most people think like you do. Thus, you assume that your own opinions are more widely held than they necessarily are. False consensus effect is common; indeed, all of us experience it at one time or another. The phenomenon is predominant among groups who share collective opinions. Interestingly, because of the false consensus effect, if you encounter someone who disagrees with your opinion, you are likely to disregard this differing opinion rather than change your own views.

Passage Notes

_____

_____

Now listen to a lecture on this topic in a sociology class.

Question 4 of 6

Lecture Notes

Question 4 of 6

Explain how the two examples discussed by the professor illustrate the false consensus effect.

Preparation Time 00:00:30
Response Time 00:01:00

Response

Task 4

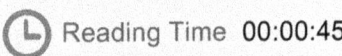

Question 4 of 6

Reading Time 00:00:45

False Consensus Effect

In sociology, the *false consensus effect* describes the tendency for people to assume that others share their beliefs. Specifically, it describes the misconception in which you assume that most people think like you do. Thus, you assume that your own opinions are more widely held than they necessarily are. False consensus effect is common; indeed, all of us experience it at one time or another. The phenomenon is predominant among groups who share collective opinions. Interestingly, because of the false consensus effect, if you encounter someone who disagrees with your opinion, you are likely to disregard this differing opinion rather than change your own views.

Passage Notes

false consensus effect

- *assuming others think like you*

Now listen to a lecture on this topic in a sociology class.

I want to give two examples of the false consensus effect so that you can better understand it. Let me give you one example that demonstrates how it affects individuals and another example to demonstrate how it affects a group that shares a collective opinion.

To start, imagine two people who have fallen madly in love with each other. At the beginning of the relationship, everything seems wonderful to both partners. Hormones and the false consensus effect blind the two people to any differences they might have. However, after several months or years of being together, the false consensus effect fades, and the two partners may have to confront their real differences. At this point, the two people can easily fall into the trap of feeling that the other is "defective" because he or she doesn't share all of the same opinions. If they're mature adults, they can work through their differences to build a stronger relationship.

Next, imagine that you decide to buy a birthday gift for your cousin, but you've only met him once before. Yet knowing that your cousin is the same age as you and enjoys reading, you decide to buy him one of your favorite books. Because of your superficial similarities to your cousin, you figure that he'll enjoy the same type of literature as you, but in reality, he may like to read completely different genres. Thus, you assume that your cousin shares your taste in literature, even though you have little evidence to support this assumption. This is another perfect example of the false consensus effect in action.

Lecture Notes

1) in love
- 1st → blind to diff.
- later → see diff. believe other = defective

2) gift for cousin
- don't know well, but cousin likes to read
- → buy book you like → false consensus effect

Question 4 of 6

Explain how the two examples discussed by the professor illustrate the false consensus effect.

 Response

The false consensus effect is the misconception that most others think like you do. Thus, when you discover that others think differently, you may disregard their opinions. The lecture gives two examples of the false consensus effect. First, the professor talks about a romantic relationship. At first, two partners are likely to ignore or fail to acknowledge their differences due to the false consensus effect. However, over time, the false consensus effect disintegrates. At that point, the two people must confront their real differences. In many cases, each person views the other partner as having the wrong opinions. Second, the professor talks about how the false consensus effect may influence a person's decisions when purchasing a gift. If I buy a gift for someone I don't know well, I'll probably get something I like for them, thinking that I must like what most others like. However, that might not be true, and the person I buy the gift for might have completely different tastes or interests.

Task 5

Listen to a conversation between two students.

Question 5 of 6

Conversation Notes

_____
_____
_____

Preparation Notes

_____
_____
_____
_____

Question 5 of 6

The students discuss two possible solutions to the man's problem. Describe the problem. Then state which solution you prefer and why.

Preparation Time   00:00:20
Response Time   00:01:00

Response

Task 5

Model Answer

Listen to a conversation between two students.

F: Hey, John. Where have you been lately? I haven't seen you all semester.

M: Oh, I thought I told you: I decided to take a little break from the university.

F: You don't strike me as the type of student who needs to "take a break" in the middle of his studies. Is there something wrong?

M: Actually, I ran out of money to pay for school.

F: You ran out of money? I thought your parents were paying for school.

M: They were, until my dad lost his job four months ago. And right now, I don't have any other choice.

F: Have you looked into taking out a student loan? They're really easy to obtain.

M: Not really. I don't want to be bogged down with payments after graduation.

F: A student loan isn't as bad as you think. The payments are super low once you graduate. And you can even defer the payments for a couple of years until you find a job.

M: Well, I didn't know that. Maybe I'll look into a student loan.

F: Also, the work-study program at this school is pretty awesome. One of my friends is doing it right now, and she's getting almost her whole tuition paid.

M: Oh, I've heard of it. How does it work?

F: You work part-time for a company in your field of study and they pay your tuition. It's kind of like an internship. The only thing is that you have to work pretty hard, from what I understand.

M: Huh, sounds interesting. I'll have to check that out, too.

F: Female Student / **M:** Male Student

Conversation Notes

problem: can't pay for school

sol. 1: student loan

sol. 2: work-study program

Preparation Notes

work-study program

* *practical: edu.+money → kill two birds*

* *benefit long term*

Question 5 of 6

The students discuss two possible solutions to the man's problem. Describe the problem. Then state which solution you prefer and why.

 Response

The man temporarily suspended his college studies because he can't afford tuition. The woman proposes two solutions for the man's problem—obtain a student loan or participate in a work-study program. In my opinion, the man should take part in the work-study program. The student loan might be a good solution to his problem because it is easy to obtain. But the man worries about repaying the loan after graduation, which I think is an understandable concern. However, the work-study program will help the man get a practical education in his field of study, so it's a good chance to gain experience for his future. Most importantly, the company may pay the man's whole tuition. Thus, pursuing a work-study program will accomplish two goals. Although the man would have to work really hard, doing so would benefit him in the long term.

Task 6

Listen to part of a lecture in a psychology class.

Question 6 of 6

Lecture Notes

Question 6 of 6

Using points and examples from the lecture, describe sleep hygiene and explain the two good sleep hygiene habits presented by the professor.

Preparation Time 00:00:20
Response Time 00:01:00

Response

Task 6

Model Answer

Listen to part of a lecture in a psychology class.

Insomnia is a common condition in which individuals experience great difficulty attaining a proper and healthy amount of sleep. For decades, doctors treated insomnia with drugs, or in many cases, not at all. However, in recent years, a new practice called "sleep hygiene" has been adopted. Sleep hygiene refers to a person's sleep-related habits and behaviors. Thus, in order to sleep well, it's important to have good sleep hygiene. This means following certain guidelines to ensure restful, effective sleep. Now let's talk about two good sleep hygiene habits. One is maintaining a calm atmosphere in your sleep area, and the other is establishing a regular bedtime.

One good sleep hygiene habit is to avoid using electronic devices in your sleep area. This usually means not having a television or computer near your bed. Believe it or not, the body and brain associate locations with activities. As a result, if your room is the primary place where you watch television or use your computer, your body and mind are likely to be "activated" every time you inhabit this location.

Another good sleep hygiene habit is establishment of a regular bedtime every night. This may seem difficult at first, especially to those with insomnia. However, studies show that one of the main ways to get an effective night's sleep is to go to bed at around the same time each night. Doing so habituates a person's body into wanting to sleep at that time each night. However, you should never go to bed unless you're tired. Individuals who only lie on their beds when tired have a much better chance of getting to sleep quickly than those who sit or lie in bed at other times of the day.

Lecture Notes

sleep hygiene

1) no distraction in sleep area

  • no TV, games, sports → body, mind activated

  • guidelines for good sleep → 2 habits

2) regular bedtime

  • study → same bed time = effective, habituate

  • but only tired

Question 6 of 6

Using points and examples from the lecture, describe sleep hygiene and explain the two good sleep hygiene habits presented by the professor.

 Response

Good sleep hygiene refers to guidelines that help a person sleep well. The professor talks about two good sleep hygiene habits: maintaining calm in the bedroom and establishing a regular bedtime. One good sleep hygiene habit is avoiding energizing activities in your sleep area. These activities include watching TV and using a computer. When people do these activities in their bedrooms, their bodies and minds will become active every time they enter their bedrooms. Another good sleep hygiene habit is to set a regular bedtime. Studies show that going to bed at the same time every night is very effective. Doing this accustoms the body to becoming tired at the same time every night. However, an important factor here is that you should go to bed only when you're sleepy.

Task 1

Question 1 of 6

What do you think would be the greatest challenge or challenges when studying abroad at a university in a foreign country? Use specific reasons and details in your response.

Preparation Time 00:00:15
Response Time 00:00:45

Notes

Response

Question 2 of 6

Some university students are supported financially by their parents, while others support themselves with part-time jobs. Which do you think is more beneficial for students and why? Use specific reasons in your answer.

Preparation Time 00:00:15
Response Time 00:00:45

Notes

Response

TASK 1

Model Answer

Question 1 of 6

What do you think would be the greatest challenge or challenges when studying abroad at a university in a foreign country? Use specific reasons and details in your response.

Notes

getting used to unfamiliar food & culture

1) used to specific meals → picky eater
   - didn't try many diff. foods

2) not familiar w/ culture outside Korea
   - afraid → inappropriate/disrespectful w/o knowing

 Response

Traveling to a new and unfamiliar place always comes with many challenges. I believe the most difficult aspects of studying abroad would be getting used to the unfamiliar food and cultural practices in a foreign country. Having grown up in a small town in South Korea, I've become used to eating very specific meals, and I haven't tried many foreign foods. As a result, I've become a very picky eater, and I think that, getting over my pickiness would be a major challenge. Moreover, I'm not familiar with any cultural practices outside of Korea, so I'm afraid that, when studying abroad, I might embarrass myself by doing an inappropriate or disrespectful thing without realizing it.

TASK 2

Model Answer

Question 2 of 6

Some university students are supported financially by their parents, while others support themselves with part-time jobs. Which do you think is more beneficial for students and why? Use specific reasons in your answer.

Notes

part time

1) over 18

  • develop independence

2) job not just for $

  • working exp.

  • manage $

 Response

Although some people prefer to have their parents support them through college, I think university students should support themselves with part-time jobs. First, I think anyone older than 18 should learn to be independent, so they must support themselves financially. For example, when I became a legal adult, my parents expected me to get a job so that I could learn about responsibility, and I think doing so has paid off for me. Moreover, having a part-time job is not entirely about earning money. It'll also give you valuable work experience before you start your real career in the future. Plus, you'll learn to manage money with the wages you earn from the part-time job. Although managing both a job and an academic career may seem hard, I'm sure that it's more beneficial in the long run.

Task 3

Question 3 of 6

⏲ Reading Time 00:00:45

University to Improve Its Bookstore Next Year

State University will build a new bookstore next year. This bookstore will be a "super store." On top of selling books, electronics, and clothing, it will also include a café. The university is building this new store for two reasons. First, the old bookstore is too small to accommodate the current student population of 30,000. It was built 40 years ago when the university had only 10,000 students. Second, the foundation of the old bookstore was damaged in last year's earthquake, so we cannot keep operating until renovations are made.

Announcement Notes

_____
_____

Now listen to two students speak about the article.

Question 3 of 6

Conversation Notes

Question 3 of 6

The male student expresses his opinion about the new bookstore proposal. State his opinion and explain the reasons he gives for holding this opinion.

Preparation Time 00:00:30
Response Time 00:01:00

Response

Task 3

Model Answer

Question 3 of 6

Reading Time 00:00:45

University to Improve Its Bookstore Next Year

State University will build a new bookstore next year. This bookstore will be a "super store." On top of selling books, electronics, and clothing, it will also include a café. The university is building this new store for two reasons. First, the old bookstore is too small to accommodate the current student population of 30,000. It was built 40 years ago when the university had only 10,000 students. Second, the foundation of the old bookstore was damaged in last year's earthquake, so we cannot keep operating until renovations are made.

Announcement Notes

proposal: build new bookstore

reasons: 1) bookstore too small   2) bookstore's foundation damaged

---

Now listen to two students speak about the article.

M: Wow, a new bookstore. Finally! I feel like the one we have now might collapse.

F: I agree. Have you been in there since the earthquake?

M: Yeah, and the building seems kind of dangerous. I actually felt like the store was moving with everyone inside. The cracks behind the cash register look big enough to fall in. I'm not going back inside that place for the rest of the year.

F: I know!

M: Also, I'm really excited that we'll finally have a café inside our bookstore.

F: I think that'll be a great addition.

M: Yeah, I think the café will be a great place to study and do homework. Not only that, but it'll be nice to have a place to browse the books before buying them. After all, there's nothing like reading a new book with a good cup of coffee.

F: I couldn't agree more.

M: Male Student / **F:** Female Student

Conversation Notes

man supports

1) abt. to fall, post-earthquake   2) café in bookstore

• feel like "moving" cracks, big → fall in   • study & homework

• read new books before buying

Question 3 of 6

The male student expresses his opinion about the new bookstore proposal. State his opinion and explain the reasons he gives for holding this opinion.

 Response

The man approves of the university's proposal to build a new bookstore to replace the old one, and he gives two reasons for his approval. First of all, he thinks that there are too many post-earthquake dangers in the old bookstore. He points out that it feels like the bookstore is moving when filled with people. And he mentions that there are really big cracks inside the bookstore. In addition, the student is happy that the new bookstore will have a café. He says that it'll be a good place to study and do homework. Additionally, he says that the café will be the perfect place to look through the books at the bookstore before purchasing them.

Task 4

Question 4 of 6

Reading Time 00:00:45

Urban Legends

Urban legends, or more accurately contemporary legends, are modern tales that generally feature mystery, horror, or humor. Although the stories may not be completely false, they are usually stories that are retold until they are distorted or exaggerated over time. When people tell urban legends, they sometimes insist that the events in the story happened to "a friend of a friend." At times, such people believe the story to be true themselves. Urban legends are often told as "cautionary tales" that end with a lesson or moral. In the United States, such stories are particularly popular among teenagers.

Passage Notes

_____

_____

Now listen to part of a lecture on this topic in a sociology class.

Question 4 of 6

Lecture Notes

Question 4 of 6

The professor gives one example of an urban legend. Describe urban legends, and explain how the example in the lecture is representative of these stories.

Preparation Time 00:00:30
Response Time 00:01:00

Response

Task 4

Model Answer

Question 4 of 6

⏱ Reading Time 00:00:45

Urban Legends

Urban legends, or more accurately contemporary legends, are modern tales that generally feature mystery, horror, or humor. Although the stories may not be completely false, they are usually stories that are retold until they are distorted or exaggerated over time. When people tell urban legends, they sometimes insist that the events in the story happened to "a friend of a friend." At times, such people believe the story to be true themselves. Urban legends are often told as "cautionary tales" that end with a lesson or moral. In the United States, such stories are particularly popular among teenagers.

Passage Notes

urban legends = modern tales (mystery, horror, humor) → exaggerated over time

• believed to be true; end with a lesson/moral

Now listen to part of a lecture on this topic in a sociology class.

Today, I'd like to give you one example of a popular urban legend. You may have already heard this story at some point in your life, and you may have even believed it to be true. Anyway, it's called "The Choking Doberman."

As the story goes, a woman returns home after spending time with her friends. When she opens the door, the woman is greeted by her pet dog, a Doberman pinscher. Unfortunately, the dog is choking on something and can't breathe. The woman rushes him to the veterinarian's office. There, the doctor tells the woman to go home and he'll call her after the surgery. The doctor discovers that the dog is choking on three human fingers. He calls the woman and tells her to leave the house immediately and to call the police. She does so. Incredibly, when the police arrive at her house, they find a burglar missing three fingers in the woman's closet.

An American literature professor documented this story in a series of books about urban legends written during the early 1980s. Interestingly, according to the professor, this story and many other urban legends may have originated in Renaissance-era Europe, but these stories have been updated to have a modern setting.

Lecture Notes

1) the choking Doberman

woman come home → dog choking → rush to vet. → doc. tell her to go home

surgery → doc. discover 3 fingers → call & tell her to leave, call police → find burglar in closet

Ren. Europe → updated to modern setting

Question 4 of 6

The professor gives one example of an urban legend. Describe urban legends, and explain how the example in the lecture is representative of these stories.

 Response

Urban legends are basically folk tales that are set in modern places. They contain exaggerated events, but people sometimes believe that they're true. The professor gives one example of an urban legend. The professor describes a story known as "The Choking Doberman. "The story is about a woman who comes home to find her dog choking, so she takes him to a veterinarian's office. The vet tells the woman to go home while he operates on the dog. After he finds three human fingers in the dog's throat, he calls the woman and tells her to call the police. When the police arrive, they find a burglar who's missing three fingers in the woman's closet. The professor says this story may be several hundred years old, but has gradually been updated.

Task 5

Listen to a conversation between a student and a college administrator.

Question 5 of 6

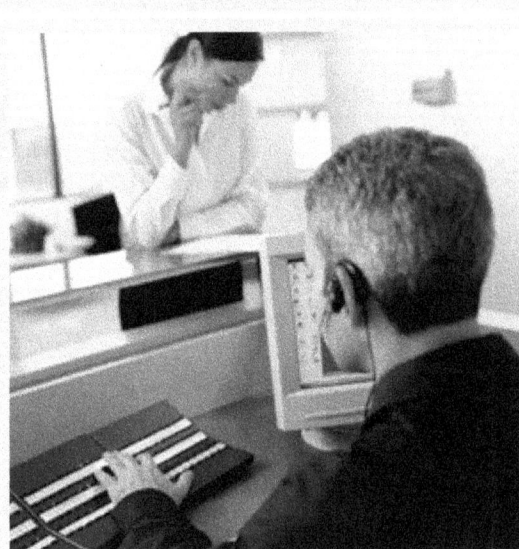

Conversation Notes

_____
_____
_____

Preparation Notes

Question 5 of 6

The administrator discusses two possible solutions to the woman's problem. Describe the problem. Then state which solution you prefer and why.

Preparation Time 00:00:20
Response Time 00:01:00

Response

Task 5

Model Answer

Listen to a conversation between a student and a college administrator.

FS: Hello. I'd like to buy a parking permit for the fall semester.

CA: Alright. A parking permit is $200 for the semester. But I must warn you that having a parking permit does not guarantee you a space in one of our lots.

FS: What are you talking about? I pay $200 and I'm not even guaranteed a parking space at one of the campus lots?

CA: Unfortunately, that's correct. Our parking lots just can't accommodate the influx of students we've had this semester.

FS: Well, what am I supposed to do, then? I live 20 miles from school, so I can't just walk here every day.

CA: One thing we're suggesting to students is that they enroll in afternoon rather than morning classes. The campus lots are crowded even in afternoons, but have relatively fewer cars at that time.

FS: Oh, okay. That's a possibility, though it could be hard because I have a job and sometimes I need to work afternoon shifts.

CA: Well then, another option is to use a free "park-and-ride" lot about one mile from campus. There are usually open spaces there. From this lot, you can catch a free shuttle bus to the campus. The only problem is that the bus stops running at 6 pm, so if you have any night classes, you'll have to walk between campus and this lot.

FS: I see. That's definitely another possibility, though I do sometimes take night classes. I guess I'll have to think about it and decide which one works better for me.

FS: Female Student / **CA:** College Administrator

Conversation Notes

problem: $200 parking permit, no guaranteed parking space

sol. 1: take afternoon classes

sol. 2: "park & ride" lot

Preparation Notes

"park & ride" lot

• free shuttle to campus

• no bus after 6 pm → walk, good exercise

Question 5 of 6

The administrator discusses two possible solutions to the woman's problem. Describe the problem. Then state which solution you prefer and why.

 Response

The woman is buying a parking permit, but the problem is that the university can't guarantee that every student will get a parking space. The man suggests two solutions to the woman's problem: enroll in afternoon classes or park in a lot about a mile away from the campus. I think the woman should use the off-campus parking lot. First, using the campus parking lots wouldn't be easy. Even if she takes afternoon classes, the woman might still have difficulty finding a parking place. Second, she has a job and may be required to work in the afternoons. Additionally, even though the shuttle stops running early, I think she can walk to the park-and-ride lot when she has night classes. A one-mile walk can actually be good exercise.

Task 6

Listen to part of a lecture in a cinematography class.

Question 6 of 6

Lecture Notes

_____
_____
_____
_____
_____
_____
_____
_____

Question 6 of 6

Using points and examples from the lecture, explain the two film techniques used in the television show *Lost*.

Preparation Time 00:00:20
Response Time 00:01:00

Response

_____
_____
_____
_____
_____
_____
_____
_____
_____
_____

TASK 6

Model Answer

Listen to part of a lecture in a cinematography class.

Good afternoon. Today, we're going to watch clips from a popular American television show called Lost, which aired from 2004 until 2010. This show demonstrates many of the film techniques you'll learn in this class. In the clips we're about to watch, you'll notice two important filmmaking techniques: the establishing shot and the flashback. I'd like to explain those to you right now so you know what to look for when you watch the clips.

Okay, so the first film technique that you'll see is called an "establishing shot." One of its main purposes is to establish the setting where a scene takes place. So one of these shots generally happens in the very first scene of a show. For example, with Lost this shot shows an island from above, the island on which Lost's main characters are stranded. The camera lingers on the scene for a moment so that viewers can see the location.

Another prominent film technique featured in Lost is called a "flashback." With the flashback technique, scenes of characters' pasts interject what's happening in their present lives. In fact, because the show is about a group of people who has survived a plane crash on an island, much of the show is devoted to scenes that flash back to their pasts. For example, one of the characters is from Iraq, and we see scenes of him in his past life as a soldier in the Iraqi Republican guard during a war.

Lecture Notes

2 film tech. in Lost

1) establishing shot: first scene → give location

- *ex) Lost → island, all stranded*

2) flashback: past → present

- *ex) Lost, used often*
- *1 char., soldier in war*

Question 6 of 6

Using points and examples from the lecture, explain the two film techniques used in the television show *Lost*.

 Response

The professor talks about two film techniques used in the American TV show called *Lost*. The first technique is called an establishing shot, and the second one is called a flashback. The establishing shot is a film and television technique that's often used at the beginning of a show to establish the setting. For example, the establishing shot of *Lost* is an overhead view of an island where the people in the show become stranded. The other filming technique, which is called a flashback, interrupts the action of the show to reveal a character's past experiences. According to the professor, flashbacks are very common in the show *Lost*, as they reveal information about the characters before they arrived on the island. For example, in one scene, we see a character's past, when he served as a soldier.

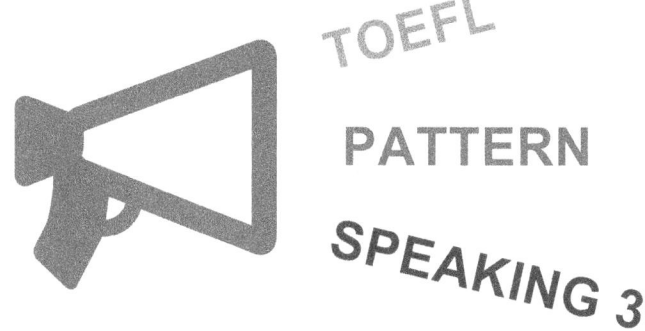

CHAPTER 8

Actual Test

TASK 1

Question 1 of 6

What do you consider the most important factors when choosing a university? Why are these factors important to you? Include examples to support your answer.

Preparation Time 00:00:15
Response Time 00:00:45

Notes

Response

Question 2 of 6

Some people think that high school students should wear uniforms to school. Others think that high school students should wear whatever they want. Which regulation do you prefer and why? Support your answer with examples.

Preparation Time 00:00:15
Response Time 00:00:45

Notes

Response

TASK 3

Question 3 of 6

 Reading Time 00:00:45

University to Change Library Policies

State University will change its library policies next semester. Instead of letting students check books out for two weeks at a time, the university will let students check books out for only one week at a time. The reasons for this action are twofold. First, over the past few years, the librarians have noticed an increased need for library materials. The student population is so large that we cannot allow students to monopolize materials for two weeks. Second, nearly 10 percent of the library materials that are checked out are never returned. The university wishes to cut this rate by at least half, and we think that this new policy will accomplish that.

Now listen to two students speak about the article.

Notes

Question 3 of 6

The male student expresses his opinion regarding the announcement. State his opinion and explain the reasons he gives for holding this opinion.

Preparation Time 00:00:30
Response Time 00:01:00

Response

TASK 4

Question 4 of 6

 Reading Time 00:00:45

Ethylene gas

Ethylene gas is a substance produced by many fruits and vegetables that causes them to ripen. Without this gas, fruits and vegetables would take a very long time to ripen. Interestingly, the more a fruit ripens, the more ethylene gas it produces. Thus, once the ripening process has started, it is difficult to slow down. Refrigeration slows ripening, but it doesn't stop the formation of ethylene gas. The most common way to prevent ripening is to harvest the fruit or vegetable before it produces large amounts of ethylene gas.

Now listen to part of a lecture on this topic in a chemistry class.

Question 4 of 6

Notes

Question 4 of 6

Using information from both the reading and the lecture, describe ethylene gas and explain how it affects the harvesting and ripening of bananas and apples.

Preparation Time 00:00:30
Response Time 00:01:00

Response

TASK 5

Listen to a conversation between a professor and a student.

Question 5 of 6

Notes

Question 5 of 6

The professor discusses two possible solutions to the man's problem. Describe the problem. Then state which solution you prefer and why.

Preparation Time 00:00:20
Response Time 00:01:00

Response

TASK 6

Listen to part of a lecture in a U.S. History class.

Question 6 of 6

Notes

Question 6 of 6

Using points and examples from the lecture, explain how western migration influenced the "American character."

Preparation Time 00:00:20
Response Time 00:01:00

Response

TASK 1

Model Answer

Question 1 of 6

What do you consider the most important factors when choosing a university? Why are these factors important to you? Include examples to support your answer.

Notes

cost & location

1) cost → not rich
   - tuition, scholarship

2) location → save $
   - live w/ parents, close
   - part-time job

 Response

For me, the biggest factors that I'd take into consideration when selecting a university are cost and location. First, I wasn't born into a wealthy family, so I simply can't afford to pay for an expensive tuition. Therefore, I would want to attend a university with low tuition fees and good scholarship programs. Moreover, selecting an affordable college now would benefit me in the future because I wouldn't have very many student loans to pay off after I graduate. Additionally, to save more money, I'd want to live with my parents. Therefore, I want to attend a university that's close to my parents' house. And it'll make it even easier for me to find part-time work in my community because I'm more familiar with the surrounding businesses.

Question 2 of 6

Some people think that high school students should wear uniforms to school. Others think that high school students should wear whatever they want. Which regulation do you prefer and why? Support your answer with examples.

Notes

uniform

(1) reduce diff. b/w poor/rich

  • shabby ↔ designer clothes

(2) no decide what to wear

  • freedom → burden

  • less tardiness

 Response

Personally, I think that high school students should be required to wear uniforms to school. First, wearing uniforms can reduce the visible gap between the rich students and the poor students. Often, I've noticed that there's a lot of tension between students when some wear old, shabby clothes while others wear new, expensive designer clothing. Introducing uniforms would help everyone look, and hopefully feel, like equals. Second, students who wear uniforms don't have to decide what to wear every morning. For some people, the freedom to choose their own clothes is actually a burden. Thus, it's easier to have just one option. Moreover, requiring uniforms might even reduce tardiness because students won't have to spend time picking out an outfit each morning.

TASK 3

Model Answer

Question 3 of 6

 Reading Time 00:00:45

University to Change Library Policies

State University will change its library policies next semester. Instead of letting students check books out for two weeks at a time, the university will let students check books out for only one week at a time. The reasons for this action are twofold. First, over the past few years, the librarians have noticed an increased need for library materials. The student population is so large that we cannot allow students to monopolize materials for two weeks. Second, nearly 10 percent of the library materials that are checked out are never returned. The university wishes to cut this rate by at least half, and we think that this new policy will accomplish that.

Now listen to two students speak about the article.

M: Did you read about this new library policy? I don't know what the administration is thinking.

F: I read about the policy, but it doesn't strike me as unreasonable.

M: It seems pretty unreasonable to me. I'm a history major, and most of my assignments take one or two months to complete. So when I check out books for those projects, I need to keep them for a long time.

F: Wow, I guess I can see how the new policy would make that hard. I'm an engineering major, so I don't really check out many books.

M: Another thing that strikes me as strange is the idea that reducing checkout periods from two weeks to one week will reduce the number of stolen items.

F: I guess the library believes that people will be more attentive with a reduced rental period.

M: But those who steal library items are going to steal unless there are severe consequences. The problem is that they obviously have little regard for school property. Reduced checkout times aren't going to help.

F: I suppose that's probably true. Maybe the administrators need to rethink this new policy.

M: Male Student / **F:** Female Student

Notes

proposal: reduce checkout time: 1 month → 1 week

man opposes

1) history major
   - check out long for projects

2) won't reduce # of stolen items
   - severe consequences
   - little regard for property

Question 3 of 6

The male student expresses his opinion regarding the announcement. State his opinion and explain the reasons he gives for holding this opinion.

 Response

The man disapproves of the university library's plan to reduce item checkout period from two weeks to one week. First of all, he says that as a history major, he needs to check books out for many weeks or months at a time to complete his class projects. This new policy will make it very difficult for him to conduct research over long periods of time. Additionally, the man says that reducing checkout times from two weeks to one week will not reduce the amount of stolen library materials. He also says that students who steal will only be deterred from doing so by severe consequences. Merely reducing checkout times won't stop those who have little regard for school property from stealing.

TASK 4

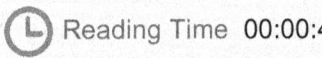

Question 4 of 6

Reading Time 00:00:45

Ethylene gas

Ethylene gas is a substance produced by many fruits and vegetables that causes them to ripen. Without this gas, fruits and vegetables would take a very long time to ripen. Interestingly, the more a fruit ripens, the more ethylene gas it produces. Thus, once the ripening process has started, it is difficult to slow down. Refrigeration slows ripening, but it doesn't stop the formation of ethylene gas. The most common way to prevent ripening is to harvest the fruit or vegetable before it produces large amounts of ethylene gas.

Now listen to part of a lecture on this topic in a chemistry class.

Let me give you two examples to illustrate how ethylene gas affects produce.

Bananas often remain green and unripe long after being home from the supermarket. They become yellow only after releasing large amounts of ethylene gas. Once the ripening process starts, the bananas release more and more of this ethylene. Consequently, this process makes the ripening process move faster. If you want bananas to ripen very quickly, put them in a plastic bag. With the ethylene gas trapped inside, they'll change color quite rapidly.

Now, let's consider the ripening process of apples. Apples are often harvested when they're unripe, before ethylene gasses are produced in large amounts. Right before they're taken to the supermarket, growers spray the apples with ethylene gas. This starts the ripening process and ensures that the apples will ripen while they're in the supermarket or once people take them home.

Notes

ethylene gas: produced by fruit, vege. → makes ripen

1) bananas

  • green @ market → release eth. → yellow

  • ripen fast → put in bag

2) apples

  • picked unripe

  • before market, spray eth. → start ripen

Question 4 of 6

Using information from both the reading and the lecture, describe ethylene gas and explain how it affects the harvesting and ripening of bananas and apples.

Response

Ethylene is a gas released by many fruits and vegetables. This chemical causes produce to ripen. In the lecture, the professor gives two examples that explain how ethylene gas is used to ripen fruits. First, the professor describes how ethylene gas affects bananas. After being picked, bananas slowly turn from green to yellow as they release ethylene gas. As time goes by, the bananas release increasingly large amounts of ethylene gas, which causes them to ripen faster. They'll ripen even faster if put in a bag because doing so traps the gas with the bananas. Next, the professor describes how ethylene gas affects apples. Growers pick apples when they're still unripe. Before arriving at the store, the apples are sprayed with ethylene gas. This spray causes them to begin ripening when they arrive in the store, or when people bring them home.

TASK 5

Model Answer

Listen to a conversation between a professor and a student.

P: Hello, Dave. You wanted to speak to me about something?

MS: Yes, Professor McMillan. I really like your teaching style, but I think this calculus class is just too hard for me. I've gotten C's and D's on every quiz. (Jokingly) Any chance you could just make the class easier?

P: (Laughs) I'm sorry, Dave. I'm afraid I can't do that. But don't worry too much; most freshmen who take the first level of my calculus series perform in the C to D range until they learn the basics.

MS: Ah. That's interesting, but I don't really want to get a C or a D on my report card, you know? It's important for me to keep my grades up.

P: I understand. There are some options you might want to consider. First off, have you checked out the university tutoring center? I hear they have excellent math tutors.

MS: Gosh, I don't know. I'm not sure if they could give me the amount of help I need.

P: Well, like I said, you're doing all right so far. I mean you're still keeping up with many other students in the class. You just need a little help from the tutors, I think.

MS: Well, I'll definitely consider some tutoring help.

P: Anyway, here is another thing you might want to consider: you could drop this class, take a pre-calculus class next semester, and then start with the calculus series next year.

MS: But then I'd be behind my classmates. I wanted to get the calculus series out of the way this year.

P: At least you'll perform better next year. Think about it.

P: Professor / **MS:** Male Student

Notes

problem: calculus class too hard → got C, D on quiz

sol. 1: go to tutoring center

sol. 2: drop, take pre-calc., start calc. next yr.

preference: go to tutoring center

- *doing fine, need little help → improve little by little*
- *may feel good to drop now, but regret later*

Question 5 of 6

The professor discusses two possible solutions to the man's problem. Describe the problem. Then state which solution you prefer and why.

 Response

The man has a problem with his calculus class. He wants to maintain good grades, but he believes that the class is too difficult for him. The professor offers him two solutions. One solution involves receiving math help at the university tutoring center. The other solution is to drop this class and take the calculus series next year. Personally, I think the man should use the tutoring center. Although the man thinks he's in a terrible situation, the professor says he's currently receiving the average grade and he just needs a little help. I think he should try the tutoring center and work to improve his grades little by little. Furthermore, if he dropped the class, I believe that he would feel relief initially, but later he would regret it because he'd be stuck in calculus next year when others have moved on to the next series of classes.

TASK 6

Model Answer

Listen to part of a lecture in a U.S. History class.

Western migration is a persistent theme in American history. First, western migration carried early European settlers across the Atlantic Ocean to North America in the early 1500s. It further compelled these settlers to journey across North America and travel all the way to the Pacific Ocean, which American settlers finally reached during the mid-1800s. Interestingly, this western migration has shaped what has shaped the so-called "American character," an ideal founded on self-reliance and democracy.

Because the western frontier was so isolated, many early migrants had to develop a kind of aggressive self-reliance. They made many of the items that people in developed regions of the country would've bought, such as homes, furniture, and tools. Many historians now believe that due to the harsh conditions present during the western migrations, Americans developed self-reliance as a cultural trait.

Another way the western migration shaped the American character was that it promoted democracy. For example, most migrants heading west were from the lower classes or most recent immigrant groups in American society. These groups of people set up simple forms of government in which everyone participated. In addition, the western frontier also offered many resources, such as gold, wood, and good hunting that were available to everyone. Both of these ideas are defining features of American democracy today.

Notes

western migration: long hard process → self-reliance, democracy

(1) self-reliance

   • *western frontier = isolated → make goods, not buy*

   • *harsh conditions*

(2) democracy

   • *migrants = lower class, new immigrants*

   • *gov. style = all participate / resources = avail. to all*

Question 6 of 6

Using points and examples from the lecture, explain how western migration influenced the "American character.".

 Response

The western migration that began in Europe and ended at the Pacific coast was a slow yet important process in American history. According to the lecture, this migration shaped two aspects of American character: self-reliance and democracy. First, the professor says the western migration made Americans more self-reliant. Because people couldn't buy many items in isolated frontiers, they had to make what they needed themselves. Additionally, facing harsh conditions as they traveled across North America helped American settlers become self-reliant. Next, the professor says the western migration promoted democracy. Most migrants to the west were from the lower classes or from among the newly arrived immigrants. They created their own kinds of government that allowed everyone to participate. In addition, the resources in the West were available to everyone. All these contributed to American democracy.

www.ingramcontent.com/pod-product-compliance
Lightning Source LLC
Chambersburg PA
CBHW080438170426
43195CB00017B/2815